COLORSTROLOGY™

Copyright © 2005, 2014 by Pantone, Inc.

Library of Congress Cataloging in Publication Number: 2013911677

ISBN: 978-1-59474-691-8

Printed in China

Typeset in Helvetica Neue

Cover design by Katie Hatz
Interior design by Andrea Stephany and Katie Hatz
Production management by John J. McGurk

Quirk Books
215 Church Street
Philadelphia, PA 19106
quirkbooks.com

10 9 8 7 6 5 4 3 2 1

COLORSTROLOGY™

WHAT YOUR BIRTHDAY COLOR SAYS ABOUT YOU

BY MICHELE BERNHARDT

ORIGINAL CONCEPT CREATED BY DANN GERSHON
IN COOPERATION WITH PANTONE, INC.

QUIRK BOOKS
PHILADELPHIA

ACKNOWLEDGMENTS

I would like to thank Dann Gershon for the ingenious concept of a birthday color calendar and for his relentless drive of the *Colorstrology* project. Thanks also to Richard Herbert, for his integrity and support; to Lisa Herbert, for her enthusiasm and sense of fair play; to Liz Vitiello, for her devotion to excellence; and to Reign Voltaire, for naming *Colorstrology*. Thanks to Samantha Seegull, who scanned for mistakes and linguistic blunders, and to Dona Ogilivie, who helped me mix and match the colors. I thank Melissa Wagner and all those at Quirk Books for their energy and commitment to making this book a huge success.

Thanks to my family and friends. Every single one of them has been a blessing and a light along the way. I thank my mother, who raised me in a home where intuition and magic were embraced, and Dayle Haddon, for many lifetimes of cherished friendship.

Words cannot convey the gratitude I feel for the angels I have in my life. You know who you are. When I think of you I am reminded that miracles happen every day.

Lastly, I would like to thank my son, Mathew, for his love and support, and my husband, Dillon, who quietly not only edits what I write but has a belief in my gift and a love of spirit that is both pure and enduring. Without them, nothing would taste as sweet or be as meaningful.

INTRODUCTION

Colorstrology combines astrology with intuitive wisdom and the metaphysical power of color to create a personal color for each day and month of the year.

The colors we see all around us are a reflection of the sun's light in all its glory. It is magic made visible. There is nothing more miraculous, unexpected, or enchanting than seeing a rainbow in the sky. You are part of that rainbow of light, and just as the particular sun sign of your birthday offers insights into your personality and nature, a personal color corresponds to the real you and reflects the very essence of the day you were born.

There is a world of possibility contained in each day of birth. There are strengths and weaknesses and gifts and challenges. You have a sun sign and a ruling planet, and you belong to a particular element—fire, earth, air, or water. Your birthday carries a numerological vibration that has a specific meaning. Each of these components shapes your personality and life experiences, and, when combined, they create the personal colors on which *Colorstrology* is based.

Just as certain astrological signs have a natural affinity for one another, so do colors. Some colors clash, whereas others are complementary. People who are born just a day apart can have distinct differences. For example, a person born on the first day of the month is likely to be dynamic and outgoing. Someone born a day later may be more sensitive and mate-oriented. *Colorstrology* reflects these innate differences.

It is important to understand that your birth color and your favorite color may or may not be one and the same. Your birth color honors the real you. A favorite color can change as you grow and evolve, and often does. It can be influenced by outside stimuli and opinions. Your birth color, however, is a constant. It is a key that connects your inner and outer worlds.

YOUR PERSONAL COLOR

There are 366 personal colors, one for each day of the year. Look up your day of birth to find a color that is unique to you. It may not be your current favorite, but it was specifically selected to honor and balance all the different parts of you.

Many people love and relate to their color naturally. However, some people may not be particularly fond of their color. Always be as open and honest as possible about how you respond to the colors. The *Colorstrology* system is designed so that everyone can use any of the colors in the manner best suited to them. Look for a color that you respond to, and add it to your environment to help bring out the essence and meaning of that particular hue.

You can incorporate your color into your life through art, clothing, or décor. Notice how it evokes specific thoughts, emotions, and feelings. Colors can be added to your life with flowers, paint-ings, and furniture. Hang a picture or wear a scarf, necktie, or other accessory. You can choose to use very little, or you can paint an entire room.

THE MONTHLY COLORS

There are twelve monthly colors, and just as you were born under a sun sign, you also belong to a special monthly color group. Like your daily color, the monthly color corresponds to your unique qualities and attributes. Wear, meditate on, or surround yourself with your monthly color to feel more connected to your destiny.

KEY WORDS

Every birth color in the calendar year is united with three key words, which resonate with you and your core personality traits. These words are like notes in the musical score of your color, and when embraced, they can be useful in attaining your goals.

PERSONAL PROFILE

The personal profile describes the essence of your particular day of birth. Use it to remind you of your true self and to feel in line with your destiny and your soul's purpose. If you are attracted to the personality profile of another birthday, you can use that color to help exemplify those qualities.

COMPATIBLE BIRTHDAYS

Each birthday lists three days that are compatible with your own. In the *Colorstrology* system, birthday color compatibility is based on the principles of color, elements, planets, and numerological affinity.

You may also find that you are at ease with people who share a color that is similar to your personal color in shade or hue (for example, January 31 and October 12). Enjoy looking up the birthdays of people you know to see what you have in common.

DIFFERENT WAYS TO USE THE SYSTEM

All the monthly colors, along with their qualities and attributes, can be useful to everyone. For instance, if you need help with relationships or want more balance in your life, you can wear, meditate on, or surround yourself with Cerulean, the color for October. If you want more prosperity in your life, work with Bud Green. And so on.

There is valuable insight to be gained by first looking up the monthly color of the person who is of interest to you, followed by his or her personal color. By combining these colors and their attributes, the essence of that particular birthday and person begins to emerge.

If you have a real attraction to a certain color, look it up and see what it represents. You can introduce that color into your environment to help you embody those qualities.

Look up dates for milestones such as graduations, promotions, anniversaries, or other meaningful events—learning about the color energy of those days can be revealing.

Colorstrology can be used for planning, too. When choosing a wedding date, for instance, you could look up different colors and their meanings to find a day that reflects the hopes and wishes of you and your mate. You can also integrate both of your personal colors at the wedding and reception.

Explore the world around you and notice the colors that other people are wearing. Look up the basic monthly color and begin to understand their motivations. For example, people who wear a lot of purple, like February's Sheer Lilac, tend to care about the community and the world.

Colorstrology is intended to be a gentle and nonjudgmental exploration of the world of color. Its purpose is to help you gain insight into your essential self while supporting you on your outward journey in life. *Colorstrology* is designed to awaken our sense of wonder, lift our spirits, and connect us to the miracle of life. We are all part of a rainbow of light, and each and every one of us is special and unique.

JANUARY

CARAMEL

PRACTICAL
DETERMINED
BUILDER

The color for the month of January is Caramel. Logical and sure-footed, this is a color of substance and determination. After the exuberance of December, we are met with the practical and down-to-earth month of January. The earth tones in Caramel help us feel stable and responsible. This color encourages us to ground our earthly ambitions through discipline and persistence.

Caramel = PANTONE 16-1439

CARAMEL can be used by anyone to help attain goals.

Caramel's essence is similar to that of the earth, which sustains and supports the growth of flowers and trees. It grounds your energy and enables you to stay focused on your objectives. Caramel helps increase patience, tenacity, and endurance—call on this color for any endeavor requiring discipline and self-control.

JANUARY

BAKED CLAY

ENTERPRISING
HUMOROUS
KEEN

If you were born on this day:
Your mind is sharp, and your intellect is keen and witty. You can use words with amazing grace, and people find your ideas and points of view stimulating and intriguing. Many people born on this day have a gift for prose and other creative arts. Trying to find a balance between being in a relationship and remaining independent can be one of your challenges.

How this color benefits you:
Your personal color helps you share your world with others without sacrificing your individuality. Wearing, meditating on, or surrounding yourself with Baked Clay reminds you to integrate your leadership abilities with spontaneity and enthusiasm.

Compatible birthdays:
March 15 • July 1 • December 30

Baked Clay = PANTONE 18-1441

TOASTED NUT

MUSICAL
EMOTIONAL
RESPONSIBLE

If you were born on this day:
The need to partner with another and to share who you are with the world is important to your evolution. Integrating your emotions with the more controlled and disciplined side of yourself is the challenge. Balance is needed for you to feel calm, worthy, and relaxed.

How this color benefits you:
Your personal color helps you combine the gentle and sensitive side of your nature with your practical and more driven side. Wearing, meditating on, or surrounding yourself with Toasted Nut helps to lighten the load while reminding you that all your innate qualities have value and worth.

Compatible birthdays:
March 12 • May 11 • November 13

Toasted Nut = PANTONE 16-1327

TOAST

LOVABLE
RELENTLESS
FUNNY

If you were born on this day:
You know what you want, and you are not afraid to go get it. You enjoy committing yourself wholeheartedly and won't settle for anything that isn't completely up to your standards. It is your ease, not your muscle, that makes people support your endeavors. Although you are charismatic and jovial, you are definitely not a pushover.

How this color benefits you:
Your personal color helps you stay on an even keel. Wearing, meditating on, or surrounding yourself with Toast reminds you to have the basics in place before you go out on a limb.

Compatible birthdays:
April 26 • May 6 • July 2

Toast = PANTONE 16-1331

COGNAC

TALENTED
STRUCTURED
CREATIVE

If you were born on this day:
Your ability to see things that others often can't is quite extraordinary. You are a builder and an architect. Whether you are designing a floor plan or brainstorming conceptual ideas, you are capable of envisioning things before they even exist. You like to do things your way. There are times, however, when you need to leave room for the opinions of others.

How this color benefits you:
Your personal color encourages you to build your dreams. Wearing, meditating on, or surrounding yourself with Cognac helps you connect with the seemingly impossible and partake in the creation of beauty.

Compatible birthdays:
July 9 • October 31 • December 25

Cognac = PANTONE 18-1421

NOSTALGIA ROSE

POWERFUL
KNOWING
EXPRESSIVE

If you were born on this day:
You are creative and talented and have an understanding of life and human nature that contributes to your wisdom. Intelligent yet emotional, you want a vehicle to help you express yourself and your ideas. Your sensitivity needs an outlet to avoid becoming isolated. The key to your happiness lies in expressing your ideas, thoughts, and feelings.

How this color benefits you:
Your personal color helps ease your mental restlessness. Wearing, meditating on, or surrounding yourself with Nostalgia Rose connects you to the greater good and mitigates emotional conflicts.

Compatible birthdays:
June 23 • October 24 • November 22

Nostalgia Rose = PANTONE 17-1512

APPLE BUTTER

HARDWORKING
THEORIST
PHILOSOPHER

If you were born on this day:
Your unique way of thinking and your perception of the world and the people in it can lead others to new ways of seeing things. Education is an important factor in your growth, and people born on this day tend to continue to study past traditional schooling. You are sensual and have a love of life and its pleasures that can be either relished or excessive.

How this color benefits you:
Your personal color helps you focus and ground your visions. Wearing, meditating on, or surrounding yourself with Apple Butter encourages you to enjoy life's pleasures without going overboard.

Compatible birthdays:
April 7 • May 14 • August 29

Apple Butter = PANTONE 18-1426

ROAN ROUGE

REFLECTIVE
INTENSE
UNIQUE

If you were born on this day:
Your quirky personality makes you
irresistible and pulls people toward
you. Your unusual take on life makes
you stand out and be noticed. This
can make you feel special or at
times a little separate from others.
Courageous in your expression, you
do well in the performing arts or any
other field that allows you to be distinct. You have a style all your own.

How this color benefits you:
Your personal color embraces your
individuality, yet supports the value
of finding your place within the
human family. Wearing, meditating
on, or surrounding yourself with Roan
Rouge helps you balance your
intensity with sweetness.

Compatible birthdays:
February 16 • August 16 •
September 2

Roan Rouge = PANTONE 18-1616

CANYON ROSE

SEXY
MUSICAL
GRAND

If you were born on this day:
Provocative and daring, you are larger than life. Born to perform and to change the status quo, you need an outlet for your creativity and gregarious personality. Your sensuality and appeal is a 10 on the Richter scale. The need to find a balance between your home life and your professional life requires both work and trust.

How this color benefits you:
Your personal color encourages you to have a stable structure to support your dreams and aspirations. Wearing, meditating on, or surrounding yourself with Canyon Rose helps you relax and appreciate every stage of your life.

Compatible birthdays:
January 16 • July 11 • September 28

Canyon Rose = PANTONE 17-1520

JANUARY 09

EARTH RED

SERIOUS
PRACTICAL
PURPOSEFUL

If you were born on this day:
You are extremely loyal to those you love. Hardworking and responsible, you like to keep things in order and get the job done. Be sure to reach out to others in times of need and stay connected to your community. Don't allow everyday pressures to take up too much of your time and energy.

How this color benefits you:
Your personal color helps you move through heartache or personal betrayal you may have experienced. It reminds you to release what doesn't work so you can move on to a more joyous opportunity. Wearing, meditating on, or surrounding yourself with Earth Red helps you combine your practicality with passion.

Compatible birthdays:
February 26 • October 28 • December 25

Earth Red = PANTONE 18-1631

BOMBAY BROWN

REALISTIC
SELF-SUFFICIENT
CREATIVE

If you were born on this day:
You have an ambitious spirit and can accomplish a great deal with a positive point of view. People born on this day know that it takes discipline, hard work, and enormous intention to achieve the high goals that you have set for yourself.

How this color benefits you:
Your personal color helps you integrate love into your everyday activities. Wearing, meditating on, or surrounding yourself with Bombay Brown stimulates optimism and reminds you to stay flexible and lighthearted as you move toward your goals.

Compatible birthdays:
April 26 • June 20 • December 10

Bombay Brown = PANTONE 18-1250

DOE

PROFOUND
AMBITIOUS
SPIRITUAL

If you were born on this day:
You have a wonderful combination of capability and perception. You know what it takes to get the job done, and you do it. You can be highly motivated and single-minded when you want to be. A spiritual belief system is important to you— it gives you strength and connects you to your soul's purpose. Practice flexibility and compassion in your interactions with others.

How this color benefits you:
Your personal color helps you share your brilliance with others. Wearing, meditating on, or surrounding yourself with Doe affirms your position in life and helps you feel secure and at peace.

Compatible birthdays:
March 3 • April 17 • May 1

Doe = PANTONE 16-1333

GINGER BREAD

IMAGINATIVE
QUICK
DILIGENT

If you were born on this day:
You are creative and artistic and have a look and a style that people find interesting. There seems to be something about you that is uniquely your own. You are often found working out or taking a yoga class. Taking care of your body is important to you. Although you can be friendly and social, you keep most of your personal feelings to yourself.

How this color benefits you:
Your personal color helps you transcend any challenges you may encounter. Wearing, meditating on, or surrounding yourself with Ginger Bread encourages compassion for yourself and others.

Compatible birthdays:
February 23 • March 21 • July 2

Ginger Bread = PANTONE 18-1244

FIR

STRIVING
PROUD
KNOWLEDGEABLE

If you were born on this day:
You have a great and valuable source of knowledge hidden within you that you may not discover until you have encountered some challenges in your life. Diligence, fortitude, and responsibility need to be developed to harness this type of power. You are goal-oriented, so it is important for you to have objectives that you love.

How this color benefits you:
Your personal color reminds you to enjoy the journey. Wearing, meditating on, or surrounding yourself with Fir can provide you with enough discipline and optimism to reach your destination and enough flexibility to change courses when it becomes necessary.

Compatible birthdays:
March 16 • June 10 • October 26

Fir = PANTONE 18-5621

ARCTIC

SMART
SOCIAL
CHARISMATIC

If you were born on this day:
You are very clever, and there isn't a social circle in which you can't hold your own. Your life is never dull, and you move easily in and out of conversations and situations. Relationships with loved ones can be challenging at times, for you are not always as self-assured on the inside as you are on the outside. Trust needs to be cultivated and developed.

How this color benefits you:
Your personal color helps restore your faith in others. Wearing, meditating on, or surrounding your-self with Arctic allows you to lead when appropriate and to follow when necessary.

Compatible birthdays:
April 6 • June 11 • July 11

Arctic = PANTONE 17-4911

CEDAR WOOD

LEADER
PERSUASIVE
SENSUAL

If you were born on this day:
You have a very strong will and are determined to get what you go after. The challenge is to know what really gives you pleasure. Although monetary worth is important to you, it is not the ultimate in regard to contentment. Try to develop a strong belief system and practice faith whenever possible. You are capable of many things.

How this color benefits you:
Your personal color helps you stay true to your inner self. Wearing, meditating on, or surrounding your-self with Cedar Wood can help you stay uplifted.

Compatible birthdays:
February 15 • September 1 • November 6

Cedar Wood = PANTONE 17-1525

BURLWOOD

INFLUENTIAL
COMMANDING
ORIGINAL

If you were born on this day:
You are quick-witted, and people seem drawn to you. You want to express your talents in significant ways. It is important that you have some private time for yourself, even though the career you choose may mean that you are surrounded by the public. Being by the water or the ocean is soothing to your spirit.

How this color benefits you:
Wearing, meditating on, or surrounding yourself with Burlwood reminds you that you do not always have to be on call for others and encourages you to reserve some quiet time for yourself.

Compatible birthdays:
February 25 • April 12 •
November 8

Burlwood = PANTONE 17-1516

TANDORI SPICE

DYNAMIC
INTRICATE
COLORFUL

If you were born on this day:
You have passion and presence and are a force to be reckoned with. Your perception and intellect are highly developed, and you are usually one step ahead of everyone else. You want to make a difference and have an impact on society, so it is important that you follow your dreams without losing your center.

How this color benefits you:
Your personal color helps accentuate your true calling. Wearing, meditating on, or surrounding yourself with Tandori Spice encourages you to rest and be receptive whenever it is appropriate.

Compatible birthdays:
April 23 • July 20 • August 1

Tandori Spice = PANTONE 18-1444

DECO ROSE

FRIENDLY
COMPASSIONATE
DETERMINED

If you were born on this day:
Your imagination and dreams help guide you toward your goals. Once you have found them, you must pursue them with persistence, flexibility, and ease. When you have had some success, you may tend to take yourself too seriously. That won't work, because it is your love of life and childlike quality that everyone relates to and admires.

How this color benefits you:
Your personal color helps you maintain your humility and honor. Wearing, meditating on, or surrounding yourself with Deco Rose helps you feel strong, safe, and truly secure.

Compatible birthdays:
March 15 • June 29 • July 2

Deco Rose = PANTONE 17-1614

LION

UNUSUAL
COMPLEX
INNOVATIVE

If you were born on this day:
You have an enormous amount of energy at your disposal. Leading others and sharing insights are just some of your abilities. The creative arts are a natural for you. You were born on the cusp of the old and new ways of doing things, so you are often part of revolutions and new ways of seeing things. Learn how to balance spontaneity with stability.

How this color benefits you:
Your personal color resonates with integration. Wearing, meditating on, or surrounding yourself with Lion helps balance your energy so you feel alive without feeling scattered or overwhelmed.

Compatible birthdays:
May 10 • July 19 • September 2

Lion = PANTONE 17-1330

LIGHT MAHOGANY

INTELLIGENT
KIND
SOCIALLY CONSCIOUS

If you were born on this day:
You care about people and yearn to make a difference. You are sensitive and bold when you need to be and will fight for the rights of others. Your mind is quick, and you are able to speak in front of an audence with an easy manner people respond to. You are able to communicate information and insights in a provocative and nonthreatening way.

How this color benefits you:
Your personal color resonates with strength and compassion and helps blend your heart with your head. Wearing, meditating on, or surrounding yourself with Light Mahogany helps you balance your home and family life with your career and professional aspirations.

Compatible birthdays:
April 16 • May 30 • September 3

Light Mahogany = PANTONE 18-1436

ZEPHYR

INTELLIGENT
WRITER
FINANCIALLY PROTECTED

If you were born on this day:
Many people born on this day have a propensity for writing. It may be easier at times to express yourself in writing instead of speaking. Your mind is highly active, so it is important for you to communicate both creatively and physically. Sports, dance, and the arts are all activities that can bring joy and help you relax.

How this color benefits you:
Your personal color helps you honor both the emotional and intellectual sides of life. Wearing, meditating on, or surrounding yourself with Zephyr encourages you to step out of your mind and into your heart.

Compatible birthdays:
May 25 • October 2 • November 3

Zephyr = PANTONE 15-1906

BLUE SURF

DEEP THINKER
SERIOUS
HIGHLY EVOLVED

If you were born on this day:
You may seem flexible on the outside, but no one can make you do something you don't want to do. You have a strong spiritual side that is the core of your essence. Earnest and responsible, you are inclined to overwork. Try not to be so hard on yourself. You are a kind and compassionate person and are highly evolved when it comes to understanding that we are all connected.

How this color benefits you:
Your personal color promotes ease and understanding, especially toward yourself. Wearing, meditating on, or surrounding yourself with Blue Surf helps you execute your ideas. It reminds you to take action and enjoy moderation.

Compatible birthdays:
March 14 • May 26 • November 27

Blue Surf = PANTONE 16-5106

PURPLE IMPRESSION

DISTINCTIVE
INTRIGUING
STYLISH

If you were born on this day:
You are quick on your feet and know how to move in and out of situations. Your mind is active and alert. It is your sense of style, however, that sets you apart from others. People love to look at you. You can set trends because of the way you dress, behave, and express yourself. You have vision and are not afraid to work hard.

How this color benefits you:
Your personal color helps you hold true to your course. Wearing, meditating on, or surrounding yourself with Purple Impression highlights your originality and strength.

Compatible birthdays:
February 24 • November 15 • December 24

Purple Impression = PANTONE 17-3919

LILAS

SENSUAL
CREATIVE
SENSITIVE

If you were born on this day:
You are creative and expressive and may have a talent for the stage or film. People born on this day tend to be larger than life. It is important for you to have a way to express yourself that is safe and nurturing. Emotions are not always rational and should not be treated with criticism or repression.

How this color benefits you:
Your personal color helps you ride the waves of life and dissolves any illusions of separateness that people can sometimes feel. Wearing, meditating on, or surrounding yourself with Lilas encourages you to reach out and connect with others.

Compatible birthdays:
February 6 • May 19 • December 15

Lilas = PANTONE 16-1708

MELLOW MAUVE

SPIRITUAL
IDEALISTIC
INTUITIVE

If you were born on this day:
You have many talents and are capable of doing a variety of things. Action and self-motivation are important. It is essential that you develop a strong sense of self and not rely too much on others. You are intuitive, and if you listen to your inner voice, you will know exactly what to do and when to do it.

How this color benefits you:
Your personal color helps you hold the reins while enjoying the journey. Wearing, meditating on, or surrounding yourself with Mellow Mauve connects you with your spiritual side and invokes a sense of trust and strength.

Compatible birthdays:
June 2 • September 8 • November 27

Mellow Mauve = PANTONE 17-1612

DUSKY ORCHID

DILIGENT
ATTRACTIVE
RESPONSIBLE

If you were born on this day:
You are capable and sure-footed
and usually know what you want
and how to get it. You are very
selective in your likes and dislikes,
especially regarding people and
relationships. You tend to be
committed once you make up your
mind on a career or a partner.

How this color benefits you:
Your personal color helps open up
any limited or restricted viewpoints
you may have. Wearing, meditating
on, or surrounding yourself with
Dusky Orchid stimulates your
creativity and interaction with others.

Compatible birthdays:
February 4 • July 26 • October 6

Dusky Orchid = PANTONE 17-1610

POLIGNAC

ADORABLE
INTERESTING
UNUSUAL

If you were born on this day: There is something about you that people just love. It may be your innocence or your unusual perception of life that keeps people enamored. You have a strong sense of what is right and wrong, and you care deeply about humanity. Friends are important to you, so be sure to surround yourself with the right people.

How this color benefits you: Your personal color resonates with your high ideals. Wearing, meditating on, or surrounding yourself with Polignac helps you see clearly and accept change with trust and optimism.

Compatible birthdays: February 27 • June 6 • November 29

Polignac = PANTONE 16-1712

LAVENDER FROST

QUIRKY
SMART
SUCCESSFUL

If you were born on this day:
You are extremely bright and may become bored if you are not stimulated or surrounded by people who can keep up with your keen intellect. Your dry sense of humor cracks people up. You can be daring and different. Although there may be times when you would like to be an average Joe, more often than not you find yourself in a fast-paced world, doing new things.

How this color benefits you:
Your personal color resonates with peace and joy. Wearing, meditating on, or surrounding yourself with Lavender Frost helps you believe in your partnerships and trust in your accomplishments.

Compatible birthdays:
May 30 • July 26 • September 10

Lavender Frost = PANTONE 15-3507

KEEPSAKE LILAC

FUNNY
TENDER
AMBITIOUS

If you were born on this day:
You were born to make a difference. It is not uncommon to find you in front of an audience. Although you are very tender on the inside, you are not afraid to go after what you want. Faith and the spiritual side of life can help you move through many obstacles. There can be a struggle between your need for partnership and your need to be alone.

How this color benefits you:
Your personal color helps you embrace intimacy. Wearing, meditating on, or surrounding yourself with Keepsake Lilac helps dissolve feelings of separateness you may have on a personal level.

Compatible birthdays:
April 11 • September 29 • October 23

Keepsake Lilac = PANTONE 15-2705

PALE MAUVE

HARDWORKING
CARING
PREPARED

If you were born on this day:
You are diligent and can be found working when everyone else has stopped. You are a natural-born advocate for human rights, and people can count on you once you have made a commitment. You have strong convictions, so it is important that you remain open to new ideas. Allow yourself to laugh as often as possible and learn to be kinder to yourself.

How this color benefits you:
Your personal color helps you find a balance between work and play. Wearing, meditating on, or surrounding yourself with Pale Mauve helps you integrate trust and flexibility with tenacity and commitment.

Compatible birthdays:
October 3 • November 11 • December 29

Pale Mauve = PANTONE 15-1607

AQUIFER

DEVOTED
BIGHEARTED
HUMANITARIAN

If you were born on this day:
You are the person to call in a time
of need. People can count on you
to rally and come through. You
have an understanding of and a
compassion for the human element
that far outweighs those of the
average person. Smart and fun to
be with, you are a favorite at any
function because of your love of life
and generosity of spirit.

How this color benefits you:
Your personal color resonates with
your high ideals. Wearing, meditating on, or surrounding yourself with
Aquifer helps you feel safe and
grounded.

Compatible birthdays:
March 31 • July 26 • August 29

Aquifer = PANTONE 15-5207

SHEER LILAC

UPLIFTING
PROGRESSIVE
DETACHED

The color for the month of February is Sheer Lilac. Inspiring and imaginative, this color invokes the qualities of humanity and kindness. Sheer Lilac helps us comprehend the spirit of humankind and allows us to experience our friends and the people in our community as family. Use this color when emotionally entangled, for it can help you practice and understand detachment.

Sheer Lilac = PANTONE 16-3617

FEBRUARY

FEBRUARY

SHEER LILAC can be used by anyone to feel a sense of belonging and global community.

Sheer Lilac inspires a loving detachment and a fresh perspective on emotional issues. It is the color that corresponds with friendship and community. Wear or surround yourself with this color when working for a cause, sharing love on a global level, or connecting to your true spiritual nature.

BURNISHED LILAC

INDEPENDENT
PERSEVERING
FOCUSED

If you were born on this day:
You have a strong independent streak and know how to do things for yourself. Making decisions, following an outline, and doing anything that is cerebral comes easily to you. It is important for you to honor the emotional side of life, especially in regard to relationships and expressing your feelings.

How this color benefits you:
Your personal color helps balance the aggressive with the sensitive side of your nature. Wearing, meditating on, or surrounding yourself with Burnished Lilac helps you to yield when necessary and increases your receptivity, flexibility, and compassion.

Compatible birthdays:
January 4 • April 8 • June 4

Burnished Lilac = PANTONE 15-1905

ORCHID HUSH

COMPASSIONATE
POETIC
ARTISTIC

If you were born on this day:
Most people born on this day are highly evolved. You have a sensitive nature that does not understand cruelty, greed, or ugliness. Artistic and kind, you can be giving to a fault. Try not to be so hard on yourself. It is vital for you to express your creative talents and to surround yourself with people who honor and respect you.

How this color benefits you:
Your personal color helps you vibrate to your highest frequency. Wearing, meditating on, or surrounding yourself with Orchid Hush helps you stay magical and lighthearted as you build your dreams into visions of glory.

Compatible birthdays:
February 28 • March 28 • December 20

Orchid Hush = PANTONE 13-3805

PERSIAN VIOLET

POIGNANT
PRECISE
TALENTED

If you were born on this day:
You have myriad talents from which to choose. Artistic and technical, you can succeed in many areas. It is important for you to contribute something to society. It is your effect on the community and the world that will give you the most pleasure.

How this color benefits you:
Your personal color helps you move through the different stages of life with ease. Wearing, meditating on, or surrounding yourself with Persian Violet reminds you to keep your individuality without distancing yourself from the people you love and who love you.

Compatible birthdays:
March 2 • November 21 • December 9

Persian Violet = PANTONE 17-3925

FEBRUARY 03

CELADON GREEN

TENACIOUS
UNUSUAL
HARDWORKING

If you were born on this day:
Although you have a good sense of humor, there can be an unusually serious side to your nature. You tend to carry more than your share of responsibility. You are determined and not afraid to work hard. You have an original way of seeing things and are never short on ideas.

How this color benefits you:
Your personal color helps you stay lighthearted as you manifest your dreams. Wearing, meditating on, or surrounding yourself with Celadon Green infuses your life with trust and enthusiasm.

Compatible birthdays:
August 4 • October 2 • November 23

Celadon Green = PANTONE 14-0114

LAVENDER LUSTRE

PROVOCATIVE
PRIVATE
ALLURING

If you were born on this day:
There is something unusual and
provocative about people born on
this day. No one really knows what
is going on inside of you. This type
of quiet or mystery that is a part of
your persona can be very compelling.
You are smart and insightful, and your
perceptive skills can be uncanny.

How this color benefits you:
Your personal color honors your
individual style while allowing you
to connect with others on an
intimate and profound level.
Wearing, meditating on, or surrounding yourself with Lavender
Lustre resonates with the higher
aspects of life and embodies the
qualities of faith and spiritual unity.

Compatible birthdays:
January 6 • March 7 • October 25

Lavender Lustre = PANTONE 16-3920

VIOLET

TRENDSETTER
SEDUCTIVE
MAGNETIC

If you were born on this day:
There is something about you that makes others sit up and take notice. People seem to gravitate to you. You have a sensual nature and know how to live life fully. Going all out is one of your gifts and also one of your challenges. It is important that you learn restraint and moderation as early as possible.

How this color benefits you:
Your personal color inspires love and joy. Wearing, meditating on, or surrounding yourself with Violet allows you to enjoy all the pleasures the world has to offer, while savoring each morsel with total presence and satisfaction.

Compatible birthdays:
January 23 • May 1 • June 24

Violet = PANTONE 16-3320

PAISLEY PURPLE

SPIRITUAL
EFFICIENT
HEALTH-ORIENTED

If you were born on this day:
You are spontaneous and energetic and can get a lot done with your exuberant personality. You are quick on your feet but can become frustrated when you have to do things in a slow and tedious way. Although you are mentally active, you also know how important it is to take care of your body. Swimming or being by the water can be very healing for you.

How this color benefits you:
Your personal color is infused with depth and passion. Wearing, meditating on, or surrounding yourself with Paisley Purple helps you calm down and honor the reflective, quieter moments in life.

Compatible birthdays:
August 7 • September 29 • December 29

Paisley Purple = PANTONE 17-3730

CROCUS

DRIVEN
QUIRKY
CHARMING

If you were born on this day:
People born on this day tend to be charming and good-looking. Although you are warmhearted, your emotions are not easy for you to handle. You have a tough exterior but a sensitive, feeling nature. You may use more energy keeping people away than you do connecting with them on an intimate level. Work and financial success usually come easily to you.

How this color benefits you:
Your personal color embodies the qualities of light and joy. Wearing, meditating on, or surrounding yourself with Crocus motivates you to connect with others on a heart level and keeps you from becoming too serious or intense.

Compatible birthdays:
March 28 • June 22 • August 28

Crocus = PANTONE 16-3115

MAUVE SHADOWS

THOROUGH
INTELLECTUAL
ADVOCATE

February 09

If you were born on this day:
You are strong and powerful and are willing to fight for a cause. You may go chin-to-chin with someone but often suffer when people are unfair or mean. You are a loyal friend, a generous partner, and far more sensitive than you appear.

How this color benefits you:
Your personal color helps you evolve through change more easily and can prevent you from developing a protective armor that can keep love and opportunity away from you. Wearing, meditating on, or surrounding yourself with Mauve Shadows helps you move through hurt feelings and come out on the other side with renewed resilience and energy.

Compatible birthdays:
May 15 • June 27 • July 2

Mauve Shadows = PANTONE 16-3205

PEACH

SMART
COMMUNICATIVE
YOUTHFUL

If you were born on this day:
Although you can be easygoing, you are not afraid to say what's on your mind when you are pushed against the wall. You may not think so, but communicating and moving in and out of social situations are things that come naturally to you. Many people born on this day can be found in the performing arts.

How this color benefits you:
Your personal color helps ease your sense of responsibility. Wearing, meditating on, or surrounding yourself with Peach helps you align with your inner calling while keeping you flexible, humble, and open to opportunities and solutions.

Compatible birthdays:
June 4 • October 7 • December 9

Peach = PANTONE 14-1227

VIOLET TULIP

EASYGOING
FRIENDLY
PLEASURE-ORIENTED

FEBRUARY 11

If you were born on this day:
You are fun to be with, laugh easily, and are intellectually acute. You like to do things in your own particular way, and it is important for you to feel safe and secure. You are both independent and mate-oriented. You enjoy doing things with others, but it is not always easy for you to share what you consider your own.

How this color benefits you:
Your personal color embraces your loving nature. Wearing, meditating on, or surrounding yourself with Violet Tulip keeps your moods balanced and your step lively.

Compatible birthdays:
February 22 • July 2 • August 12

Violet Tulip = PANTONE 16-3823

WISTERIA

COMMUNICATIVE
HUMANITARIAN
BUSINESS ACUMEN

If you were born on this day:
You have a good sense of style, romantic flair, and a head for business. You are mentally active, but relationship issues take up much of your thought process. Once you commit yourself, you have a tendency to love fully.

How this color benefits you:
Your personal color reminds you to believe in yourself. Wearing, meditating on, or surrounding your-self with Wisteria helps dissolve any feelings of self-doubt. It enables you to trust that the perfect partner will see the beauty that is uniquely yours and love you for it.

Compatible birthdays:
July 14 • August 23 • December 30

Wisteria = PANTONE 16-3810

LAUREL GREEN

LIVELY
ENDURING
CREATIVE

If you were born on this day:
You have a strong presence that is felt by others. When you walk into a room, people know it. Your persona and your confident manner often mean you are seen as an authority. Although you have a gift for making people laugh, you are not as light-hearted as you may seem.

How this color benefits you:
Your personal color helps you handle the challenges that come your way with more ease and optimism. Wearing, meditating on, or surrounding yourself with Laurel Green helps keep your heart open and dissolves any urge to be defensive or sarcastic.

Compatible birthdays:
April 11 • June 18 • December 24

Laurel Green = PANTONE 15-6313

VISTA BLUE

FUNNY
UNUSUAL
RESTLESS

If you were born on this day:
You march to your own drumbeat, and no amount of pestering will change your course until you decide to do so. You are agreeable and friendly but prefer to do things your own way. Once you have an idea or a purpose in mind, you can be relentless in your pursuit of it. No one can ever call you average.

How this color benefits you:
Your personal color helps you discern fact from fiction. Wearing, meditating on, or surrounding yourself with Vista Blue helps keep you open-minded and eases any mental restlessness you may experience.

Compatible birthdays:
May 7 • July 5 • August 14

Vista Blue = PANTONE 15-3930

LUPINE

KIND
SENSITIVE
SMART

If you were born on this day:
You are kind and loving and are an excellent friend. You know how to listen and how to support others because of your own sensitivity. Your creative intelligence should be channeled and supported.

How this color benefits you:
Your personal color helps you stay in the game even when you see and hear things that are contrary to your nature. Wearing, meditating on, or surrounding yourself with Lupine helps you move through the emotional wounds of life without losing your loving and beautiful spirit.

Compatible birthdays:
January 14 • March 15 • December 21

Lupine = PANTONE 16-3521

LAVENDULA

POWERFUL
THEATRICAL
DRIVEN

If you were born on this day:
You are enthusiastic and theatrical in your expression. You are very talented and need to follow your dreams. The challenge often lies in how to do so. Some people born on this day try so hard that they tend to buck the system, and others find it difficult to try at all. Balancing desire, sensitivity, and action is the key to this situation.

How this color benefits you:
You are usually honest, even to a fault, and your personal color helps balance your exciting personality. Wearing, meditating on, or surrounding yourself with Lavendula helps calm your nerves as you gain perspective.

Compatible birthdays:
May 11 • June 19 • July 22

Lavendula = PANTONE 15-3620

DUSTY LAVENDER

TALENTED
FIGHTER
SENSITIVE

If you were born on this day:
Whether it is music, sports, or fighting for a cause, you are always up to the task. You have an unusual combination of sensitivity and might. This sensitivity, when properly channeled, affords you many possibilities. When you feel offended, you can sometimes lose your perspective and miss the opportunities that the universe is offering.

How this color benefits you:
Your personal color combines the qualities of passion and detachment. Wearing, meditating on, or surrounding yourself with Dusty Lavender helps you remain open and forgiving as you move through the emotional aspects of life.

Compatible birthdays:
January 2 • May 24 • August 3

Dusty Lavender = PANTONE 17-3313

ORCHID HAZE

CHARISMATIC
INTELLIGENT
PRINCIPLED

If you were born on this day:
You are intelligent and highly principled. You want to do the right thing and believe in being conscious about what you say and do. Your mind is quick, and it is important that you surround yourself with people who are intelligent and non-judgmental. You feel empowered when you care for your body in a disciplined and loving manner.

How this color benefits you:
Your personal color helps you feel connected with others. Wearing, meditating on, or surrounding yourself with Orchid Haze helps you feel balanced and confident.

Compatible birthdays:
March 18 • August 21 • October 20

Orchid Haze = PANTONE 16-2107

BLUSH

IMAGINATIVE
INSTINCTIVE
KNOWLEDGEABLE

If you were born on this day:
You love to learn and explore new things, especially if there is an artistic or organic slant to the subject. Although you get along well with others, you have a strong independent streak. You want a partner with whom you can share your life, but one who doesn't require all your energy.

How this color benefits you:
Your personal color helps you express the passionate and spontaneous side of your nature. Wearing, meditating on, or surrounding yourself with Blush allows you the freedom to nurture your own soul and explore intriguing horizons.

Compatible birthdays:
April 3 • May 25 • November 29

Blush = PANTONE 15-1614

LAVENDER AURA

PROFOUND
EMOTIONAL
TRANSFORMING

If you were born on this day:
Many people born on this day have had to overcome their share of obstacles. You are able to move through many of life's challenges and transform the difficulties you encounter into gifts of insight and wisdom. You have the ability to convey the emotional impact of life in a way that others can see without necessarily having to live through it themselves.

How this color benefits you:
Your personal color helps you transform adversity into fortune. Wearing, meditating on, or surrounding yourself with Lavender Aura teaches you how to let go of the old and embrace the new.

Compatible birthdays:
July 22 • August 11 • October 29

Lavender Aura = PANTONE 16-3911

LAVENDER MIST

WRITER
CREATIVE
EMOTIONAL

If you were born on this day:
You have a unique and private side to your personality, and you tend to be emotionally complex. You can grasp ideas and concepts that most people can't wrap their minds around. You are often able to express yourself in a public forum more readily than on a personal level. Resist the urge to blame yourself or others for any apparent misfortune. This type of thinking will only drain your energy and impede your growth.

How this color benefits you:
Your personal color helps you be more objective. Wearing, meditating on, or surrounding yourself with Lavender Mist lifts your spirit and highlights your talents.

Compatible birthdays:
April 10 • May 13 • June 11

Lavender Mist = PANTONE 16-3307

CAMEO GREEN

UNDERSTANDING CONCEPTUAL APPEALING

If you were born on this day:
You have an understanding of the human condition that few people possess. You are compassionate and care about the world and the people in it. You are giving and supportive in relation to your friends and the community. You are able to do many things on an emotional and intellectual level.

How this color benefits you:
Your personal color reminds you to take care of your own needs as well as the needs of others. Wearing, meditating on, or surrounding yourself with Cameo Green helps you ground your vision for humanity into something concrete and tangible.

Compatible birthdays:
January 23 • June 3 • October 30

Cameo Green = PANTONE 14-6312

FOREVER BLUE

PROVOCATIVE
SELF-ASSURED
TROUBLESHOOTER

If you were born on this day:
You are a good decision maker. People can come to you when they have a problem because they know that you can fix it. You function best in a position of authority, where you have the ability to take care of things. It is important that you are surrounded by people who love and support you.

How this color benefits you:
Your personal color resonates with vision and expansion. Wearing, meditating on, or surrounding yourself with Forever Blue helps you stay loving in the face of change and open to new ideas and solutions.

Compatible birthdays:
April 21 • May 26 • June 26

Forever Blue = PANTONE 16-4019

PINK NECTAR

SENSITIVE
TALENTED
AESTHETIC

If you were born on this day:
You have a soft spot when it comes to loving and caring for people who are close to you. Trying to find a balance between taking care of yourself and the needs of others can be one of your challenges. You are usually good at anything related to the arts or creativity.

How this color benefits you:
Your personal color helps you express your love without becoming too attached. Wearing, meditating on, or surrounding yourself with Pink Nectar accentuates your beautiful spirit and allows you to enjoy the treasures that life brings your way.

Compatible birthdays:
February 4 • May 6 • November 4

Pink Nectar = PANTONE 14-2305

SWEET LAVENDER

PRIVATE
HUMANITARIAN
DEDICATED

If you were born on this day:
You are not afraid to fight for your beliefs. You work hard, especially if what you are doing helps people, animals, or the world. Due to your sensitive nature, you need a certain amount of time to yourself in which you can recharge and replenish your energy.

How this color benefits you:
Your personal color connects you with the sweetness that life has to offer. Wearing, meditating on, or surrounding yourself with Sweet Lavender helps you pursue your dreams in a loving manner.

Compatible birthdays:
August 29 • November 5 • December 27

Sweet Lavender = PANTONE 16-3931

CHALK VIOLET

KIND
COMMITTED
DETAILED

If you were born on this day:
Once you commit yourself to something, it is important to you that you do it well. This is in regard to both relationships and work. You can be hard on yourself and others, especially if the people around you are careless or lazy. You want to feel passionate about something and support this passion with action.

How this color benefits you:
Your personal color lends sensitivity to your strength. Wearing, meditating on, or surrounding yourself with Chalk Violet helps you transform any hurts or wounds you may experience into a depth of understanding and a desire to live life more truthfully and lovingly.

Compatible birthdays:
July 4 • September 10 • November 6

Chalk Violet = PANTONE 17-3615

VIOLET QUARTZ

ENDEARING
TALENTED
FAIR

If you were born on this day:
People find you easy to be around. You are a kind and loving person and have an understanding of human nature that is both perceptive and compassionate. You laugh easily and give people plenty of room to be themselves. You have a high regard for what is right and fair. You have a lot of talent and need to be loved and adored.

How this color benefits you:
Your personal color gives you the strength necessary to pursue your dreams. Wearing, meditating on, or surrounding yourself with Violet Quartz supports your physical body with energy and vitality.

Compatible birthdays:
March 13 • June 21 • September 1

Violet Quartz = PANTONE 18-1720

ORCHID MIST

DETERMINED
ENERGETIC
FUN LOVING

If you were born on this day:
You are not afraid to work hard.
Many people born on this day are
made for the limelight and love to
be in front of an audience. You are
warm and generous, and once you
commit yourself to someone or
something, it can be difficult for you
to change course. Your tenacity
and will often get you where you
want to go.

How this color benefits you:
Your personal color reminds you to
take care of yourself. Wearing,
meditating on, or surrounding yourself with Orchid Mist helps you relax
and care for your body in a moder-
ate and loving manner.

Compatible birthdays:
April 1 • May 23 • August 28

Orchid Mist = PANTONE 17-3612

ASHLEY BLUE

GIFTED
PARTNER ORIENTED
INTUITIVE

FEBRUARY 29

If you were born on this day:
Most people born on this day are very artistic and intuitive. You have a refined nature, and you understand what it means to be subtle or unobtrusive. You have a silent presence that is indicative of your innate wisdom. You can be hurt easily because of your sensitive nature. Try not to hide or distance yourself from others.

How this color benefits you:
Your personal color helps you move through fear and self-doubt. Wearing, meditating on, or surrounding yourself with Ashley Blue infuses wisdom and vision into your daily interactions.

Compatible birthdays:
May 1 • July 31 • November 18

Ashley Blue = PANTONE 16-4013

MARCH

FAIR AQUA

INTUITIVE
SUBTLE
EMPATHETIC

The color for the month of March is Fair Aqua. Dreamy and illusive, this color helps guide people between the conscious and subconscious worlds. Fair Aqua evokes the qualities of trust and clarity. Neptune, god of the oceans, presides over the month of March.

Fair Aqua = PANTONE 12-5409

FAIR AQUA can be used by anyone to aid trust and recall childlike wonder.

Fair Aqua can lift your spirits when life seems too drab or mundane. It is a color that evokes inspiration and intuition. Meditate with this color in mind when you need help identifying your innermost desires or are feeling a lack of imagination. Wear or surround yourself with Fair Aqua as an aid to sleeping, dreaming, and meditating.

MARCH

PISTACHIO GREEN

INSPIRATIONAL
ARTISTIC
DETERMINED

If you were born on this day:
You have a never-ending spring of talent and creativity. It is vital for you to create and inspire others. Your optimism and strong sense of purpose allow you to move past obstacles and negative opinions.

How this color benefits you:
Your personal color helps you stay centered and acknowledge your own gifts. Wearing, meditating on, or surrounding yourself with Pistachio Green supports your physical vitality and aids you in the manifestation of your dreams and aspirations.

Compatible birthdays:
January 6 • June 10 • December 11

Pistachio Green = PANTONE 13-0221

BAY ○

EMOTIONAL
CREATIVE
HIGHLY PRINCIPLED

If you were born on this day:
There is a strong creative spirit in people born on this day. You have high ideals and are not afraid to make them a reality. Some of you have a natural talent for finance. Born to promote fairness and help others, you may find yourself involved in the arts or in a humanitarian field.

How this color benefits you:
Your personal color helps ease your nerves. Wearing, meditating on, or surrounding yourself with Bay enables you to make sacrifices for a cause without draining all your energy.

Compatible birthdays:
February 3 • July 6 • August 29

Bay = PANTONE 12-5507

ROSE TAN

MENTALLY ACTIVE
COMMUNICATOR
IMAGINATIVE

If you were born on this day:
You have a gift for writing and conceptual design. Many people born on this day are involved with some form of charity. Your mind is naturally active, so you do not need an excess of caffeine or stimulants. Try not to let your vivid imagination turn into worry or negative thought patterns.

How this color benefits you:
Your personal color helps balance the mental, emotional, and physical aspects of your being. Wearing, meditating on, or surrounding yourself with Rose Tan helps you focus and direct your creative talents toward the greater good.

Compatible birthdays:
January 11 • November 10 • December 21

Rose Tan = PANTONE 16-1511

RESEDA

SPIRITUAL
PRIVATE
PRODUCTIVE

If you were born on this day:
You are capable of carrying a lot of responsibility. You have the necessary discipline to accomplish whatever it is you set out to do as long as you avoid feelings of hopelessness.

How this color benefits you:
Your personal color reminds you of your creative and innovative spirit. Wearing, meditating on, or surrounding yourself with Reseda appeals to the spiritual side of your nature. It generates courage and optimism and assists you in reaching your goals with a strong sense of peace and accomplishment.

Compatible birthdays:
March 30 • June 10 • September 16

Reseda = PANTONE 15-6414

BLUE LIGHT

SMART
CHARISMATIC
UNUSUAL

If you were born on this day:
You have a deep and profound understanding of life. Few people know the real you, because you keep a lot to yourself. Although you are a great communicator, you still have many thoughts and ideas that you cannot explain to others. You have a talent for understanding and appreciating art and beauty. Your creative abilities are many and can be exceptional.

How this color benefits you:
Wearing, meditating on, or sur-rounding yourself with Blue Light helps ease your doubts about love and reminds you to share your life with others.

Compatible birthdays:
April 5 • October 3 • December 24

Blue Light = PANTONE 13-4909

PASTEL LAVENDER

PERCEPTIVE
PARTICULAR
ATTRACTIVE

If you were born on this day:
Although you are sensitive and highly creative, it is your intelligence and keen sense of awareness that people often notice first. Not much can get past you. You have a good eye for beauty and notice the little things that others often miss. If you do not practice a little detachment and compassion, your emotions can get the best of you.

How this color benefits you:
Your personal color keeps you from distancing yourself from others. Wearing, meditating on, or surrounding yourself with Pastel Lavender helps you embrace love. It centers you and allows you to move through your feelings with trust and ease.

Compatible birthdays:
January 9 • May 24 • December 20

Pastel Lavender = PANTONE 14-3209

DAWN PINK

ARTISTIC
SENSITIVE
INNOVATIVE

If you were born on this day:
You have a good sense of artistry and design. Creative endeavors come naturally to you, especially if you have not ignored or under-valued these inherent traits. Many people born on this day work on healing emotional wounds from either childhood or family-related issues. Using your hands for heal-ing, the arts, or creating beauty is just one of the gifts you can share with others.

How this color benefits you:
Your personal color helps refresh your spirit. Wearing, meditating on, or surrounding yourself with Dawn Pink increases your faith and enthusiasm.

Compatible birthdays:
April 17 • June 12 • December 19

Dawn Pink = PANTONE 15-2205

MAUVE MIST ○

GOOD-NATURED
PRODUCTIVE
SPIRITUALLY STRONG

If you were born on this day:
You have a strong spiritual side that can be a great source of strength when channeled properly. You were meant to do something that has meaning and value. Try not to let material concerns bog you down. Focus your sense of responsibility toward high ideals and aspirations. Cultivate discipline and self-effort early on to avoid losing your footing later on in life.

How this color benefits you:
Your personal color resonates with your spiritual integrity. Wearing, meditating on, or surrounding yourself with Mauve Mist is uplifting and helps you sustain a positive and healthy outlook.

Compatible birthdays:
January 1 • April 8 • May 3

Mauve Mist = PANTONE 15-3207

MELLOW ROSE

FEISTY
UNIQUE
INTELLIGENT

If you were born on this day:
You were born with a beautiful combination of strength and sensitivity, intellect and insight. The challenge for you arises when one trait tries to muscle out the other. You are meant to find balance and live honestly while honoring both the spiritual and mundane worlds.

How this color benefits you:
Your personal color enhances your true vision and calms your mind. Wearing, meditating on, or surrounding yourself with Mellow Rose helps you feel gratitude for the gifts and the challenges you were given.

Compatible birthdays:
October 8 • November 1 • December 3

Mellow Rose = PANTONE 15-1515

MELLOW GREEN

KIND
DEEP
TALENTED

MARCH 10

If you were born on this day:
It is very important that you demonstrate your talents. It is the expression of this talent and energy in the world that will help you feel most vital and alive. You can be highly emotional because of your depth and your empathy for others.

How this color benefits you:
Your personal color allows for your compassion to stand out but shocks you out of the tendency for too much sacrifice. Wearing, meditating on, or surrounding yourself with Mellow Green helps you stay grounded while attracting financial opportunities.

Compatible birthdays:
January 3 • April 1 • December 8

Mellow Green = PANTONE 12-0426

WINTER SKY

TALENTED
AESTHETIC
RESOURCEFUL

If you were born on this day:
You were given a rare combination of artistic creativity and financial know-how. It is a wonderful gift to be able to create your dreams while building a financial structure to support them. It is important that you share your talent and your wealth with others, because it is the sharing that will bring you some of the most worthwhile blessings.

How this color benefits you:
Your personal color helps you stay centered. Wearing, meditating on, or surrounding yourself with Winter Sky infuses your life with faith and magic.

Compatible birthdays:
June 1 • July 15 • September 11

Winter Sky = PANTONE 14-4307

ALMOST APRICOT

MUSICAL
COMMUNICATIVE
EXPRESSIVE

If you were born on this day:
You were born to communicate and express your colorful personality. Many people born on this day have a talent for music, dance, or drama. You have a strong spiritual side that needs to be cultivated so that you can handle some of the challenges that life often brings.

How this color benefits you:
Your personal color lends you optimism and courage. Wearing, meditating on, or surrounding your-self with Almost Apricot connects you with the love and discipline necessary for you to feel safe and secure.

Compatible birthdays:
May 10 • June 18 • November 3

Almost Apricot = PANTONE 15-1319

MARCH 12

PASTEL GREEN

EARNEST
COMPASSIONATE
MAGICAL

If you were born on this day: Your nature is one of honesty and truth. You are a compassionate and fair person who fights for the rights of others. You have a great imagination and are willing to work hard to manifest your inspirational ideas. Take some time for yourself to replenish your energy. Dancing, having a creative business, praying, and meditating are all activities that can feed your spirit.

How this color benefits you: Your personal color helps you feel alive and energized. Wearing, meditating on, or surrounding yourself with Pastel Green reminds you to live your life in a magical and wondrous way.

Compatible birthdays: January 15 • April 15 • July 6

Pastel Green = PANTONE 13-0116

MISTY LILAC

INSPIRED
CHARMING
VIVACIOUS

If you were born on this day:
People born on this day are sociable and inspiring. You have a particular intelligence that is quite astounding. It is not a normal intellect that you possess but an uncanny ability to read people and situations that makes you wise and profound. Healing, dance, music, and the arts are just some of the areas where you can excel.

How this color benefits you:
Your personal color helps you move through your emotions with ease and understanding. Wearing, meditating on, or surrounding yourself with Misty Lilac invokes clarity and compassion.

Compatible birthdays:
January 22 • May 26 • July 7

Misty Lilac = PANTONE 15-3807

CASHMERE BLUE

SWEET
SENSUAL
SMART

If you were born on this day:
Most people find you magnetic
and lovable. You have a gentle
manner that makes you a favorite
to be around. You have an ease
that makes others feel calm. You
are quick-minded but keep much
of what you know to yourself.

How this color benefits you:
Highly sensual, your personal color
helps you guard against going to
extremes. Wearing, meditating
on, or surrounding yourself with
Cashmere Blue rekindles your spirit
and reminds you to take some time
for yourself.

Compatible birthdays:
February 16 • April 12 • September 6

Cashmere Blue = PANTONE 14-4115

THISTLE

HELPFUL
CURATOR
ANIMAL LOVER

If you were born on this day:
A lot of people born on this day do great things with their lives. You are often involved with charitable organizations. You want to lend a helping hand whether you are fighting for artistic causes or the rights of animals. Some of the difficult lessons in your life involve your own immediate family.

How this color benefits you:
Your personal color helps you release hurt feelings and old wounds. Wearing, meditating on, or surrounding yourself with Thistle combats self-doubt. It reminds you to embrace each new day with a renewed sense of wonder.

Compatible birthdays:
February 7 • November 16 • December 26

Thistle = PANTONE 14-3907

VIOLET TULLE

EXCITING
POWERFUL
SEDUCTIVE

If you were born on this day:
You are charming and fun to be around. You can be the life of the party and very exciting to watch. Many people born on this day have a sensual and seductive nature. Money, sex, spirituality, and love all need to be integrated for you to feel calm and balanced.

How this color benefits you:
Your personal color tempers your personality so that you can express your power and charisma in a balanced and sincere way. Wearing, meditating on, or surrounding yourself with Violet Tulle helps you connect with your inner self while sharing your experiences with others.

Compatible birthdays:
March 29 • May 25 • December 11

Violet Tulle = PANTONE 16-3416

MUTED CLAY ○

PROFOUND
HEALER
SPIRITUAL

If you were born on this day:
Making a contribution to humankind
is important to you. Having a spiritual
connection and being of service
helps you feel alive and balanced.
There is a greatness that is inherent
in your nature. You are generous
and care for others so much
that you may be inclined to
forget about your own needs.

How this color benefits you:
Your personal color helps you take
care of yourself as well as others.
Wearing, meditating on, or
surrounding yourself with Muted
Clay grounds your nature and
reminds you to eat well, exercise,
and love both your body and
your spiritual nature.

Compatible birthdays:
April 30 • October 26 • December 14

Muted Clay = PANTONE 16-1330

ARCADIAN GREEN

POWERFUL
EXCITING
SENSITIVE

If you were born on this day:
The ability to excel and shine is often seen early in those born on this day. You have an array of talents to choose from, including music, dance, martial arts, and drama. You have a combination of youthfulness and wisdom that is intriguing and attractive. Wise and strong, you can be a great leader and teacher if you so choose.

How this color benefits you:
Your personal color helps you balance your need for financial security with spiritual fulfillment. Wearing, meditating on, or surrounding yourself with Arcadian Green helps you stay true to your highest nature.

Compatible birthdays:
June 1 • September 6 • November 3

Arcadian Green = PANTONE 14-0123

DUSTY JADE GREEN

PERCEPTIVE
STORYTELLER
QUESTIONER

If you were born on this day:
You are not afraid to be unusual or different and are willing to stand up for your beliefs. It is vital that you have a spiritual or soulful connection in life. A mundane existence will sap your spirit and energy. It is important for you to continue to believe. Never let cynicism or negative feelings interfere with your storytelling and your gift for communication.

How this color benefits you:
Your personal color helps ease your emotional nature. Wearing, meditating on, or surrounding yourself with Dusty Jade Green helps ignite your sense of humor and replenish your spirit.

Compatible birthdays:
April 7 • April 30 • October 5

Dusty Jade Green = PANTONE 15-5711

BASIL

INNOVATIVE
EXPRESSIVE
ORIGINATOR

If you were born on this day:
You are likable and fun to have around. You seem to know what position to play when you are interacting with other people. You have a quiet self-assurance that lends you ease in communicating or dealing with others. It is important for you to be active and to learn new things.

How this color benefits you:
Your personal color embodies life and vitality. Wearing, meditating on, or surrounding yourself with Basil keeps you young and thriving. It can also be a strong aid when dealing with finances and health concerns.

Compatible birthdays:
September 30 • November 21 • December 25

Basil = PANTONE 16-6216

PURPLE ASH

STYLISH
PROUD
DYNAMIC

If you were born on this day:
You have a great sense of style, and people find you interesting and direct. You don't like to beat around the bush. You are usually financially protected. Being emotionally available is not always easy, and you are sometimes innocent and youthful in relationships.

How this color benefits you:
Your personal color reminds you to stay connected to the spiritual side of your life. Wearing, meditating on, or surrounding yourself with Purple Ash helps you trust that you are lovable. It reminds you to stay simple, honest, and true when dealing with the world and the people around you.

Compatible birthdays:
February 22 • March 11 • April 8

Purple Ash = PANTONE 17-3810

STORM BLUE

PERCEPTIVE
TALENTED
QUICK-MINDED

If you were born on this day:
You are perceptive and can read most situations and people quickly. You have an active intellect, and it is easy for you to take on anything you put your mind to. It is important for you to take action. Making mistakes is vital to spiritual growth and will move you forward only if you do not become fixated on disappointments.

How this color benefits you:
Your personal color helps you ride the emotional waves of life. Wearing, meditating on, or surrounding yourself with Storm Blue helps you stay flexible and open to new possibilities.

Compatible birthdays:
April 23 • August 2 • October 25

Storm Blue = PANTONE 17-4716

MARCH 24

MAUVEWOOD

LOVING
ROMANTIC
ARTISTIC

If you were born on this day:
There is something about your physical presence that is commanding yet likable. People often come to you for your opinion or a listening ear. You have artistic ability and a great sense of style. You have an interesting combination of compassion and courage. Doing something creative helps you express your active emotional life.

How this color benefits you:
Your personal color helps you release pent-up feelings. Wearing, meditating on, or surrounding yourself with Mauvewood gives you the courage and detachment necessary to pursue your ambitions and desires.

Compatible birthdays:
February 24 • June 4 • December 6

Mauvewood = PANTONE 17-1522

MARCH 25

BERRY CONSERVE

HEALER
INDEPENDENT
PERFORMER

If you were born on this day:
People are drawn to your magnetic
personality. You have a good sense
of humor and are not afraid to laugh
at yourself. Whether you know it or
not, you have an ability to help and
heal others. Just being around you
or listening to your words can have
a soothing effect on people. Although
you are independent, you are also
sensitive and can be withdrawn
when it comes to your own feelings.

How this color benefits you:
Wearing, meditating on, or surrounding yourself with Berry Conserve
helps you direct your energy. It
makes you feel safe without the
need for isolation or defensive
behavior patterns.

Compatible birthdays:
January 17 • May 20 • June 21

Berry Conserve = PANTONE 18-3013

WISTFUL MAUVE

SMART
PERCEPTIVE
LOYAL

MARCH 26

If you were born on this day:
You are a wonderful friend and ally, and anyone can benefit from having you in their life. You are extremely resourceful and know how to take the lead and get the job done. You are honest and profound. It can be hard for you to hold your tongue when it comes to telling it like it is.

How this color benefits you:
Your personal color helps you balance the emotional and intellectual sides of life. Wearing, meditating on, or surrounding yourself with Wistful Mauve enables you to lead without force. It helps you dance and interact with people in a beautiful and rhythmic way.

Compatible birthdays:
February 11 • March 14 • August 29

Wistful Mauve = PANTONE 17-1511

BRUSCHETTA

NEGOTIATOR
FRIENDLY
COURAGEOUS

If you were born on this day:
You have a charm people easily recognize and warm to. You are constantly on the move and crave stimulation and goals. Life seems to move quickly for you, and you tend to like excitement and a sense of challenge. Your mind is sharp and active, and when you are feeling centered, you can negotiate almost anything.

How this color benefits you:
Your personal color helps ground your energy. Wearing, meditating on, or surrounding yourself with Bruschetta helps you direct your intention while enjoying the process as well as the goals.

Compatible birthdays:
February 7 • June 9 • December 20

Bruschetta = PANTONE 18-1346

SIERRA

THINKER
HARDWORKING
ACTIVIST

MARCH 28

If you were born on this day:
When you have a cause to believe in and fight for, you are at your happiest. You are intelligent and get bored easily if you are not stimulated. You are willing to work hard and can sometimes miss the timing of things.

How this color benefits you:
Your personal color reminds you that you don't have to do everything yourself. Wearing, meditating on, or surrounding yourself with Sierra enhances your sense of timing, thereby helping you to feel safe and secure.

Compatible birthdays:
April 4 • June 1 • September 4

Sierra = PANTONE 18-1239

OIL BLUE

INTERESTING
CHARISMATIC
SEDUCTIVE

If you were born on this day:
Your charm and magnetism can take you far. You can talk anyone into just about anything. You have a spiritual side that must be cultivated. Your connections with people are very important, so pick your partnerships with care.

How this color benefits you:
Your personal color helps you keep your faith and optimism. Wearing, meditating on, or surrounding yourself with Oil Blue helps you connect with your innate wisdom. It helps you see the difference between hope and fantasy.

Compatible birthdays:
February 2 • June 11 • November 2

Oil Blue = PANTONE 17-5111

FADED ROSE

STORYTELLER
THINKER
MESSENGER

If you were born on this day:
People born on this day tend to teach others through the stories they share. Whether you are singing a song, writing a play, or painting a picture, you are able to convey images and emotions that can affect others. It is very important for you to communicate and stay active. Your thoughts can turn to worry if you are not expressing yourself and connecting with the world at large.

How this color benefits you:
Your personal color embodies love, passion, and courage. Wearing, meditating on, or surrounding yourself with Faded Rose lends you courage and enthusiasm as you connect with others and find your place in the circle of life.

Compatible birthdays:
April 6 • May 1 • December 9

Faded Rose = PANTONE 18-1629

JACARANDA

CAPABLE
KIND
INSTINCTIVE

If you were born on this day:
You know how to get the job done. You are not afraid of hard work and can carry more than your share of responsibility. You have a good sense of humor and are a kind and loving partner and friend. Being by the water is often helpful to your sense of well-being.

How this color benefits you:
Your personal color reminds you when it is time to take care of yourself and when it is time to compromise. Wearing, meditating on, or surrounding yourself with Jacaranda helps you stay strong and centered as you pursue your goals and aspirations.

Compatible birthdays:
April 2 • May 25 • October 3

Jacaranda = PANTONE 17-3930

CAYENNE

FIERY
ENERGETIC
COURAGEOUS

The color for the month of April is Cayenne. Fiery and energetic, this color signifies passion, strength, and courage. Mars, the ruling planet of Aries, governs the heavens during the month of April. We have just entered the spring season, during which there is promise of growth and plenty, and everything is new and popping with excitement. This is a time for new beginnings and initiating action.

Cayenne = PANTONE 18-1651

APRIL

CAYENNE can be used by anyone to increase energy and pizzazz.

Cayenne inspires courage and fearlessness. It supports your enthusiasm and desire to win and can give you a competitive edge in sporting events. Use Cayenne to stimulate your metabolism, enhance your vitality, and increase self-confidence. It is a great color to wear when working out or engaging in a physical activity.

FIERY RED

ENTERPRISING
VISIONARY
LEADER

APRIL 01

If you were born on this day:
You have come into this world to
be a leader. You are active and
lively and want to stand out and
express your unique point of view.
It is important for you to develop
independence and to try new
things. You are innovative and
enterprising, and you have the
ability to manifest your will if
you stay centered.

How this color benefits you:
Your personal color helps you
combine your visionary abilities
with a strong sense of purpose.
Wearing, meditating on, or surrounding yourself with Fiery Red helps you
stay courageous and enthusiastic as
you move toward your quests.

Compatible birthdays:
May 20 • June 16 • October 25

Fiery Red = PANTONE 18-1664

RAPTURE ROSE

SENSUAL
RESOURCEFUL
DRAMATIC

If you were born on this day:
A combination of strength and sensitivity is associated with this birthday. People born on this day want to live life on the edge. You are charismatic and resourceful. Although you are mate-oriented, it is important that you develop a strong sense of self, or you may find yourself in challenging situations that force you to take action and become independent.

How this color benefits you:
Your personal color helps you integrate the quality of assertion with tenderness. Wearing, meditating on, or surrounding yourself with Rapture Rose enables you to make firm decisions and assists you in following through on your goals.

Compatible birthdays:
May 6 • June 11 • December 2

Rapture Rose = PANTONE 17-1929

CHERRY TOMATO

EXPRESSIVE
GIVING
COMMUNICATOR

APRIL 03

If you were born on this day:
Your urge to communicate is strong. You have a full range of emotions that need to be expressed. Generous and courageous, you are not afraid to lend a helping hand. It is important for you to stay physically active to avoid feeling moody and disconnected from others. Being by the water, especially the ocean, can be healing.

How this color benefits you:
Your personal color helps balance any restlessness you may be feeling. Wearing, meditating on, or surrounding yourself with Cherry Tomato helps integrate the outgoing side of your personality with the spiritual and quiet side.

Compatible birthdays:
March 5 • June 1 • December 24

Cherry Tomato = PANTONE 17-1563

TRUE RED

PRACTICAL
INDUSTRIOUS
PERSISTENT

If you were born on this day:
You are strong and have a robust sense of purpose. Stable and practical, you have the ability to manifest your ideas and aspirations. Resist the tendency to be stubborn and try not to let material concerns give you a heavy heart.

How this color benefits you:
Your personal color helps you combine perseverance with the ability to stay lighthearted and flexible. Wearing, meditating on, or surrounding yourself with True Red kindles trust and blessings in regard to finances and relationships.

Compatible birthdays:
March 8 • June 22 • December 5

True Red = PANTONE 19-1664

ORANGE.COM

DYNAMIC
CHARISMATIC
DETERMINED

If you were born on this day:
You have a lot of drive and determination. Speaking to the masses suits you; you have a strong calling to communicate to large audiences. Sharing ideas with others, having fun, and staying young at heart are some of the ways to harness the magical abilities that you have within.

How this color benefits you:
Wearing, meditating on, or surrounding yourself with Orange.com helps ground your ambitions and can prevent you from scattering your energies.

Compatible birthdays:
February 5 • August 10 • October 23

Orange.com = PANTONE 18-1561

APRIL 05

BEETROOT PURPLE

IMAGINATIVE
MAGNETIC
EXPLORATIVE

If you were born on this day:
You are sensitive and creative, and there may be times when you don't feel like a typical Aries or a fire sign. Your strong, feeling nature works for you in the performing arts and in showing empathy to others. Guard against giving too much in relationships or going to excess with food, alcohol, or exercise.

How this color benefits you:
Your personal color helps you forge new relationships. Wearing, meditating on, or surrounding yourself with Beetroot Purple helps you move through any fear or uncertainty that you may feel toward the new and unexplored.

Compatible birthdays:
February 23 • May 26 • November 5

Beetroot Purple = PANTONE 18-2143

SKYWAY

SPIRITUAL
CONFIDENT
AESTHETIC

If you were born on this day:
There is a strong spiritual side to your birthday, and many people who are born on this day have healing hands and abilities. Although you can be feisty and self-assured on the outside, there is a tenderness and sensitivity on the inside. You have refined tastes, and you want to be around things of beauty. Music and the arts will help you connect with your inner spirit. Time spent by the ocean can be especially helpful.

How this color benefits you:
Wearing, meditating on, or surrounding yourself with Skyway honors the passionate side of your personality while enabling you to hear the aesthetic and spiritual calling that awaits you.

Compatible birthdays:
January 6 • July 11 • October 6

Skyway = PANTONE 14-4112

SKI PATROL

DEEP
STIMULATING
POWERFUL

If you were born on this day:
There is more to you than meets the eye. The casual and superficial are not for you. You want to connect on a deep level and get to the heart of the matter. You are magnetic and attractive to others, and you may be known for your sex appeal. Powerful and passionate, you have the ability to transform yourself and others.

How this color benefits you:
Your personal color reminds you of your inner wisdom. Wearing, meditating on, or surrounding yourself with Ski Patrol gives you the drive to communicate while initiating growth and change.

Compatible birthdays:
January 16 • March 8 • October 29

Ski Patrol = PANTONE 18-1761

POPPY RED

PERSUASIVE
ENTHUSIASTIC
EASYGOING

If you were born on this day:
The need for greatness and doing things in a big way is inherent in the personality of this birthday. It is important to build a foundation that can support your dreams and visions. Move through the necessary steps so that you can grow and cultivate your talents. Giving something of value to others will rekindle the light of your flame.

How this color benefits you:
Wearing, meditating on, or surrounding yourself with Poppy Red gives you the patience to sustain your striking vision and the trust to move past any obstacles.

Compatible birthdays:
February 11 • May 9 • June 13

Poppy Red = PANTONE 17-1664

VERMILLION ORANGE

CHILDLIKE
RELENTLESS
UNUSUAL

If you were born on this day:
You are a welcome addition to any group of people or social gathering. Perceptive and smart, you have an interesting blend of childlike wonder and intellectual prowess. You are a collector of inspiring ideas and are able to communicate information that can help light the way for others.

How this color benefits you:
Your personal color helps you to clear your head of worry and needless bits of information. Wearing, meditating on, or surrounding yourself with Vermillion Orange reminds you to take time for yourself and breathe before you go back out into the world to share your ideas and vision.

Compatible birthdays:
January 27 • February 26 • August 4

Vermillion Orange = PANTONE 16-1362

SANGRIA

INTUITIVE
THEATRICAL
INTELLIGENT

APRIL 11

If you were born on this day:
You are intuitive and insightful
and tend to be financially blessed.
Theatrical and eloquent, you are
a great storyteller. You are mate-
oriented but have to be self-
sustaining and independent
for your relationships to work.

How this color benefits you:
Your personal color inspires you to
channel your creativity. Wearing,
meditating on, or surrounding
yourself with Sangria encourages
you to take action and helps you
balance the mental, emotional, and
physical aspects of your nature.

Compatible birthdays:
January 24 • June 5 • December 7

Sangria = PANTONE 19-2047

GERANIUM

ARTICULATE
DYNAMIC
COMMUNICATOR

If you were born on this day:
You have a talent for communication, sales, and writing. You are creative and dynamic and want to express your ideas and aspirations. Travel and publishing are two areas that can offer you growth and good fortune. Be sure to take some time out to replenish your energies.

How this color benefits you:
Your personal color helps you relax. It balances your nervous system so that you know when to interact with others and when to retreat and rejuvenate. Wearing, meditating on, or surrounding yourself with Geranium helps you to focus your intensity out into the world in a creative and healthy manner.

Compatible birthdays:
March 13 • June 7 • July 25

Geranium = PANTONE 17-1753

ROCOCO RED

CREATIVE BUILDER
PERSISTENT
INFLUENTIAL

APRIL 13

If you were born on this day:
You are independent and strong-willed and can accomplish great things. You are more serious and grounded than most people know. It is important that you build and develop a solid foundation from which you can grow.

How this color benefits you:
Your personal color activates the powerful side of your nature. Wearing, meditating on, or surrounding yourself with Rococo Red encourages you to channel the life force you have within and then share your success with the world around you.

Compatible birthdays:
February 8 • June 11 • July 13

Rococo Red = PANTONE 18-1652

HIBISCUS

DETERMINED
PERSUASIVE
SPARKLY

If you were born on this day:
You have a sparkly personality; the room lights up when you are in it. It is important for you to express your ideas with flair and gusto. Staying within the status quo and being average are not for you. Remain detached in regard to material ambitions, and you will find that money and financial gain will come more readily to you.

How this color benefits you:
Your personal color gives you the staying power to follow things through to completion. Wearing, meditating on, or surrounding yourself with Hibiscus helps you listen better while improving your timing.

Compatible birthdays:
July 9 • September 5 • October 9

Hibiscus = PANTONE 18-1762

CERISE

SEDUCTIVE
SENSITIVE
ORGANIZED

If you were born on this day:
You have an array of talents, and few people can resist your charm and beauty. You are sensual and charismatic and can influence others. Being creative and organized helps you feel grounded. There can be a tendency to go to extremes, and you may swing from going overboard to becoming overly disciplined.

How this color benefits you:
Your personal color encourages you to express your abilities fully. Wearing, meditating on, or surrounding yourself with Cerise helps you balance your provocative nature and attain your rightful place in life.

Compatible birthdays:
January 3 • March 19 • July 6

Cerise = PANTONE 19-1955

APRIL 16

VIRTUAL PINK

EXPLORER
RESTLESS
SPIRITUAL

If you were born on this day:
You have passion and sensitivity coupled with a strong spiritual side. Time spent by the ocean can help quiet your mind so that you can hear your inner calling. You have a natural healing ability and can recover from ailments more quickly than most. You have a tendency to try many things in relation to career goals.

How this color benefits you:
Your personal color helps blend your courage with intelligence. Wearing, meditating on, or surrounding yourself with Virtual Pink reminds you that the journey is an essential part of the outcome and that each endeavor has its rewards.

Compatible birthdays:
January 22 • October 4 • December 7

Virtual Pink ~ PANTONE 18-1856

RIBBON RED

TENACIOUS
RESPONSIBLE
PURPOSEFUL

APRIL 17

If you were born on this day:
Powerful and strong, you are capable of managing a lot of responsibility. You are perceptive and have good investigative powers. You can use your financial insights to help others. Writing, psychology, or money-related careers are just some of the areas in life where you can excel.

How this color benefits you:
Your personal color inspires optimism and creativity whenever you are feeling separate or somber. Wearing, meditating on, or surrounding yourself with Ribbon Red assists in blending your serious side with the more lighthearted part of your nature.

Compatible birthdays:
May 16 • July 13 • December 3

Ribbon Red – PANTONE 18-1662

CRIMSON

COMMANDING
INTERESTING
ENDURING

If you were born on this day:
People born on this day have a lot of influence and strength. You are a formidable foe, and there is much that you can accomplish when you channel your energy. Trust and ease are two qualities to cultivate. Practicing the art of receiving and allowing things to come to you are ways to develop these traits. Love, rather than force, will set you free.

How this color benefits you:
Your personal color reminds you to tune in to things that you love while following your aspirations. Wearing, meditating on, or surrounding yourself with Crimson helps temper the intensity and power of your ambitions.

Compatible birthdays:
March 9 • October 22 • November 27

Crimson = PANTONE 19-1762

HIGH RISK RED

ELOQUENT
PERFORMER
AMBITIOUS

APRIL 19

If you were born on this day:
You have an ability to inspire others and know how to communicate words and feelings with style and grace. Your leadership ability and confidence make you a favorite among friends and colleagues. Resist the urge to be dominating or stubborn. You can remain young and healthy by staying active and open to new ideas.

How this color benefits you:
Your personal color encourages flexibility. Wearing, meditating on, or surrounding yourself with High Risk Red increases vitality and accentuates your star quality.

Compatible birthdays:
January 13 • July 13 • December 5

High Risk Red = PANTONE 18-1763

APRIL 20

AFRICAN VIOLET

IMAGINATIVE
EMOTIONAL
HARDWORKING

If you were born on this day:
Sensitive and strong, you are an
unusual character. You are a born
artist and a compassionate soul
who can easily be hurt by criticism.
A strong spiritual calling must be
heeded to prevent blocking off
your feeling nature by escaping
or overindulging.

How this color benefits you:
Your personal color enables you to
share your creativity and talent with
others. Wearing, meditating on, or
surrounding yourself with African
Violet helps bring good things your
way and allows your magnetism to
temper the force of your will.

Compatible birthdays:
February 22 • May 15 •
November 6

African Violet = PANTONE 16-3520

OPERA MAUVE

AMBITIOUS
DEALMAKER
STOIC

If you were born on this day:
Knowledge is very important to you. You like to learn and relay information. You are persuasive, and people often like you and look to you for guidance. You are visual and have a good eye for beauty and art. Making deals and being social may come easily to you.

How this color benefits you:
Your personal color stimulates your optimism and encourages you to rest and take a vacation from time to time. Wearing, meditating on, or surrounding yourself with Opera Mauve helps you know when to interact with others and when to spend some time alone.

Compatible birthdays:
May 3 • June 3 • November 7

Opera Mauve = PANTONE 16-3116

DARK PURPLE

COMMANDING
CONFIDENT
FUNNY

If you were born on this day:
You have a commanding personality, and people notice you when you walk into the room. Stability, security, and a little bit of spice need to be in place for you to feel settled. Being your own boss is vital to your well-being. Owning something, such as your own home or business, brings comfort and a sense of permanence. Many people born on this day have a great sense of humor.

How this color benefits you:
Wearing, meditating on, or surrounding yourself with Dark Purple reminds you not to take things too seriously and urges you toward kindness and transformation.

Compatible birthdays:
March 8 • June 4 • August 8

Dark Purple = PANTONE 19-2524

LAVENDER HERB

GIFTED
INDEPENDENT
COMMUNICATOR

If you were born on this day:
You are communicative and expressive and like to share your ideas. You have a youthful quality and can be quite adorable if you so choose. Musical ability and storytelling are just some of the talents that you may possess. It is important for you to remain spontaneous and playful. Develop both patience and tenacity to ensure a steady climb toward your aspirations.

How this color benefits you:
Wearing, meditating on, or surrounding yourself with Lavender Herb helps balance your passion and will with compromise and understanding.

Compatible birthdays:
January 31 • April 14 • July 25

Lavender Herb = PANTONE 16-3310

ULTRAMARINE

CREATIVE
RESPONSIBLE
NURTURING

If you were born on this day:
You are creative and talented and can achieve success and monetary wealth by connecting your abilities with action. The performing arts are a good vehicle for you, and many people born on this day have lovely voices. Sensual and attractive, you are capable of pulling good things toward you. Being in a loving relationship is vital to your well-being, and you need someone who is attentive and devoted.

How this color benefits you:
Your personal color helps to balance your moods. Wearing, meditating on, or surrounding yourself with Ultramarine integrates your need for artistic freedom with financial security.

Compatible birthdays:
June 22 • October 24 • November 19

Ultramarine = PANTONE 17-4037

AZURE BLUE

SOULFUL
CHARISMATIC
INTENSE

If you were born on this day:
You are kind and spiritual and want to connect to something greater than yourself. There is a strong calling to do something helpful and meaningful. You may have healing ability. Touch is very important to you, and so is being by the water. Artistic and theatrical, you are able to convey strong emotions.

How this color benefits you:
Your personal color connects you to the calm of the sea. Wearing, meditating on, or surrounding yourself with Azure Blue helps you move through the tides of change without feeling overwhelmed or lost.

Compatible birthdays:
February 7 • June 28 • November 7

Azure Blue = PANTONE 17-4139

IBIS ROSE

STRIVING
CLEVER
SPONTANEOUS

If you were born on this day:
You are clever, dramatic, and deep. Like a detective, you can find out things that other people often miss. Your ability to transform yourself and others is profound. Financial security is important to you. Resist the urge to obsess or get stuck in limiting circumstances. Your depth of feeling can at times be overwhelming.

How this color benefits you:
Your personal color combines the passion of red with the detachment of purple. Wearing, meditating on, or surrounding yourself with Ibis Rose enables you to share your insightful perceptions without getting bogged down by too many emotions.

Compatible birthdays:
January 3 • May 13 • October 3

Ibis Rose = PANTONE 17-2520

EASTER EGG

VERBALLY STRONG
STRIKING
MOTIVATED

If you were born on this day:
Action is required to achieve your ambitions. Excitement and stability need to blend together for you to make the most of your talents and desires. The urge to do something great is hidden in your birthday. Connecting with a universal cause helps you move through inhibitions.

How this color benefits you:
Your personal color helps you get past any self-defeating ideas that you may have. Wearing, meditating on, or surrounding yourself with Easter Egg combines your dedication with optimism and conviction.

Compatible birthdays:
June 25 • July 9 • August 22

Easter Egg = PANTONE 16-3925

NORTH SEA

LEADER
IDEALISTIC
VISIONARY

If you were born on this day:
The urge to create is an essential part of your nature. You have the gift of intuition and are able to communicate your ideas with inspiration and conviction. The partnerships you form can be both overwhelming and transforming. Cooperation and sensitivity are needed as you move through your everyday encounters and interactions.

How this color benefits you:
Your personal color stimulates the leader in you. Wearing, meditating on, or surrounding yourself with North Sea helps you explore new ideas and ideologies in an innovative yet secure manner.

Compatible birthdays:
March 1 • July 10 • November 5

North Sea = PANTONE 18-5115

DEEP PERIWINKLE

INSTINCTIVE
STYLISH
POIGNANT

If you were born on this day:
Manifesting your dreams is important to you. There is a strong spiritual side to your personality. Living well and being surrounded by things of beauty will lift your spirits. Try not to juggle too much or get stuck in indecision. If you stay true to yourself, you can excel and become a master in your own right.

How this color benefits you:
Your personal color helps you move through any feelings of restlessness and allows you to commit and go deeply into the areas that interest you most. Wearing, meditating on, or surrounding yourself with Deep Periwinkle helps you feel safe and secure in your intimate relationships.

Compatible birthdays:
January 11 • July 11 • November 6

Deep Periwinkle = PANTONE 17-3932

ASTER PURPLE

PERCEPTIVE
UNUSUAL
INTELLIGENT

If you were born on this day:
You are instinctive yet rational and want to be surrounded by people who appreciate your perception and enthusiasm. There is much that you can accomplish with your creativity and ability to communicate easily. Time alone near the ocean can calm your nervous system and help integrate your intuitive spirit.

How this color benefits you:
Your personal color helps you balance your creative aspirations while attracting material benefits. Wearing, meditating on, or surrounding yourself with Aster Purple supports you during challenging times and reminds you of the joy you feel when you share your wealth and sense of adventure with others.

Compatible birthdays:
June 3 • July 13 • November 4

Aster Purple = PANTONE 17-3826

BUD GREEN

HEALING
REJUVENATING
PROSPEROUS

MAY

The color for the month of May is Bud Green. Vital and assuring, this is the color of stability and healing. Bud Green opens the heart and rejuvenates the spirit. The sun moves through the earth sign of Taurus during the month of May. This earthy quality is prevalent as the color green springs into action after the bleakness of winter and graces us with its presence. Bud Green gives us a balance of strength and substance.

Bud Green = PANTONE 15-6442

MAY

BUD GREEN can be used by anyone to balance and support the physical body.

Bud Green resonates with life's riches. It corresponds with nature and can be both physically and emotionally healing. Wear or surround yourself with this color to increase prosperity and promote material wealth. It opens the heart to the true fortune of following your soul's purpose and making it manifest.

SHAMROCK

PROLIFIC
EXPRESSIVE
DYNAMIC

MAY 01

If you were born on this day:
You have a unique presence, and people take notice when you are in the room. Your ability to express yourself and convey ideas only magnifies your allure. You are open to new experiences and like to be on the move. No matter how far you travel, however, a restful home to come back to is important.

How this color benefits you:
Your personal color carries the qualities of stability and expansion. Wearing, meditating on, or surrounding yourself with Shamrock helps you feel peaceful as you move through life and explore new horizons.

Compatible birthdays:
April 6 • July 6 • October 29

Shamrock = PANTONE 15-6432

SHALE GREEN

NOTICEABLE
CURIOUS
COMMUNICATIVE

If you were born on this day:
Attractive and engaging, the energy in the air is charged when you are around. As outgoing as you may seem, you also have a significant inner life that not everyone sees or can share. Juggling two distinct parts of your personality can keep you on your toes.

How this color benefits you:
Your personal color helps integrate the sensitive and cautious side of your nature with your childlike enthusiasm. Wearing, meditating on, or surrounding yourself with Shale Green helps you feel secure as you interact with others and move toward your dreams.

Compatible birthdays:
February 7 • March 5 • November 22

Shale Green = PANTONE 16-6116

JUNIPER

ATTRACTIVE
KIND
INTRIGUING

If you were born on this day:
You are talented in so many areas
that it can be a challenge deciding
just what area to pursue. There is
a lot that goes on underneath the
social persona that you present to
the world. You have an active imagination and carry many thoughts and
ideas that you are trying to understand and assimilate.

How this color benefits you:
Your personal color helps you feel
steady and safe as you make
important decisions. Wearing,
meditating on, or surrounding
yourself with Juniper helps dissolve
any judgmental attitudes that
may inhibit your growth.

Compatible birthdays:
February 24 • July 21 •
November 3

Juniper = PANTONE 18-6330

VINEYARD GREEN

GROUNDED
LOYAL
SEARCHING

If you were born on this day:
People may look at you in awe as
you move through your daily
activities. You can handle some of
the most stressful situations with
calm and grace. You are persistent
and loyal but still need to have fun.
Dancing and interacting with
lighthearted people offers you
fulfillment and happiness.

How this color benefits you:
Your personal color symbolizes
prosperity and growth. Wearing,
meditating on, or surrounding yourself with Vineyard Green helps you
feel grounded as you search for
answers to some of life's most
important questions.

Compatible birthdays:
March 14 • April 19 • June 21

Vineyard Green = PANTONE 18-0117

KELLY GREEN

VERSATILE
PROFOUND
TALENTED

If you were born on this day:
You have an array of talents from which to choose. People find you attractive, charismatic, and interesting. You have a strong will and can be very convincing.

How this color benefits you:
Your personal color helps you integrate joy with stability. Wearing, meditating on, or surrounding yourself with Kelly Green allows you to honor any phase of life that you are encountering. It reminds you to place equal value on both your inner development and your outer position in society, including professional merits.

Compatible birthdays:
July 1 • August 1 • November 5

Kelly Green = PANTONE 16-6138

GREEN EYES

SENSUAL
FRIENDLY
SUCCESSFUL

If you were born on this day:
You are sensual and friendly and
are a desired addition to any party
or social gathering. You are fun to
be around. Talking and connecting
with others is a favorite pastime of
yours. You can be very scientific or
extremely creative and usually
have a knack for both.

How this color benefits you:
Your personal color helps nurture
your creative talents. Wearing,
meditating on, or surrounding
yourself with Green Eyes can help
direct you toward finding your
perfect mate and temper
any inclinations to go to excess.

Compatible birthdays:
February 6 • June 30 • November 6

Green Eyes = PANTONE 16-0224

CRÈME DE MENTHE
HEALER
COMMITTED
VISIONARY

If you were born on this day:
It is not uncommon for people born on this day to have a gift for healing, and very often it is the gift of touch. You may or may not be aware of this special talent, but either way, you can have quite an impact on others. You are not afraid to commit to something, and once you do, it can be difficult for you to give it up.

How this color benefits you:
Your personal color brings out the beautiful side of your nature. Wearing, meditating on, or surrounding yourself with Crème de Menthe resonates with your divine spirit. It helps you stay connected to the truth and open to change.

Compatible birthdays:
February 10 • August 7 • October 6

Crème de Menthe = PANTONE 16-5919

GARDEN GREEN

STRONG
DEEP
RESPONSIBLE

If you were born on this day:
People can feel your power when you are in a room. You have a strong sense of purpose and are not a lightweight by any means. Not only are you deep, but you have the ability to understand ideas and feelings that are complex. You can be ambitious and driven when you have set your sights on a goal.

How this color benefits you:
Your personal color corresponds with peace and depth. Wearing, meditating on, or surrounding yourself with Garden Green is nurturing to your mind, body, and spirit in a healthy and harmonious way.

Compatible birthdays:
June 4 • August 2 • September 8

Garden Green = PANTONE 19-0230

WINTER GREEN

ASSURED
LARGER THAN LIFE
CREATIVE

If you were born on this day:
You have a lot of energy, and there is a noticeable difference when you are at a gathering. When your heart is in something, you are unstoppable. You have to love what you do. You are expressive and theatrical and are often found on the stage performing for others. People find you attractive.

How this color benefits you:
Your personal color enhances your communication skills. Wearing, meditating on, or surrounding yourself with Winter Green helps you stay lighthearted and calm as you encounter emotional situations.

Compatible birthdays:
February 14 • June 30 • September 17

Winter Green = PANTONE 16-5924

KIWI

ACTIVE
DETERMINED
DYNAMIC

If you were born on this day:
People born on this day are usually active and athletic. The need to express yourself physically is important. Your body and your spirit need to be on the move, whether through dance, horseback riding, or sports. Once you put your mind to something, it is difficult for you to change course.

How this color benefits you:
Your personal color resonates with ease and flexibility. Wearing, meditating on, or surrounding yourself with Kiwi helps you move through moments of uncertainty with trust and compassion for yourself and others.

Compatible birthdays:
January 1 • April 20 • July 10

Kiwi = PANTONE 16-0235

GREEN TEA

UNUSUAL
ARTISTIC
SPIRITUAL

If you were born on this day:
You have come into this life to do something important and meaningful. You have a vivid imagination and can see new ideas and concepts more readily than others. Incorporate the spiritual side of life into your daily activities. You have a desire for independence coupled with a need to partner with someone.

How this color benefits you:
Your personal color encourages ease while finding financial security and spiritual fulfillment. Wearing, meditating on, or surrounding yourself with Green Tea promotes faith and trust in your communications with others and your pursuits in life.

Compatible birthdays:
March 31 • November 24 • December 20

Green Tea = PANTONE 15-6428

CALLA GREEN

PROFOUND
WISE
RESPONSIBLE

If you were born on this day:
You are a force to be reckoned with. You have a strong character and will not take a back seat to anyone. Being true to yourself is extremely important. You are curious and have a way with words. Seeing what is hidden under the surface is one of your gifts.

How this color benefits you:
Your personal color helps you express and communicate your perceptions in a detached and profound manner. Wearing, meditating on, or surrounding yourself with Calla Green can help you integrate love with money.

Compatible birthdays:
April 12 • June 15 • September 23

Calla Green = PANTONE 18-0435

PIQUANT GREEN

SOLID
INTERESTING
PERSISTENT

If you were born on this day:
There is something unusual and provocative about you. People find you interesting and attractive. You are solid and persistent and continue to pursue when others give up. You know how to progress toward your goals. You will be asked to change and adapt to different situations as you move through life.

How this color benefits you:
Your personal color helps you change with the times. Wearing, meditating on, or surrounding yourself with Piquant Green reminds you that there are different ways to achieve your desires and that the skills you acquire on the journey enrich you as much as arriving at your destination.

Compatible birthdays:
January 9 • June 21 • August 19

Piquant Green = PANTONE 17-0235

DEEP MINT

PROGRESSIVE
HARDWORKING
ENTERPRISING

If you were born on this day:
You are progressive and like to do things your own way. You are not afraid to work hard and may find that you are still going strong when others have gone to bed. The universe is supportive of your enterprising abilities. Strike out on your own, and express your ideas in different creative venues.

How this color benefits you:
Your personal color helps bridge the old and the new. Wearing, meditating on, or surrounding yourself with Deep Mint helps you to stay calm and understanding as you drive your ambitions forward.

Compatible birthdays:
June 10 • August 15 • November 14

Deep Mint = PANTONE 17-5937

LAVENDER GRAY

CREATIVE
MUSICAL
CHARMING

If you were born on this day:
You are a joy to be around, and everyone loves you. Creative in just about every way, you will have many choices regarding career and hobbies. Most likely you can sing, dance, or play a musical instrument, and sometimes you can do all three. The challenge comes when you try to integrate the practical side of your personality with the creative and sensual side of your nature.

How this color benefits you:
Wearing, meditating on, or surrounding yourself with Lavender Gray helps you stay centered as you find a way to channel your talents into something joyful and lucrative.

Compatible birthdays:
February 27 • June 2 • November 2

Lavender Gray = PANTONE 17-3910

WOODROSE

EXCITING
CAPTIVATING
PROVOCATIVE

If you were born on this day:
Your personality is captivating and provocative. You are a winner and can go to great heights if you stay focused. Don't let monetary concerns drain your vitality. Discipline and balance are needed for you to handle the amount of energy that moves through your body.

How this color benefits you:
Your personal color helps you control the more excitable part of your nature. Wearing, meditating on, or surrounding yourself with Woodrose heightens your spiritual awareness and connects you to a higher purpose.

Compatible birthdays:
February 10 • September 5 • November 10

Woodrose = PANTONE 16-1806

HENNA

COMMITTED
DEPENDABLE
DRIVEN

If you were born on this day:
You often feel driven and have a definite mission in life. You take on your desires with complete conviction and fervor. Although you are passionate, you also have a gentle quality that people may not see. You are intuitive and have an awareness that can be used to direct and achieve your goals. Your home life is important to you.

How this color benefits you:
Your personal color helps you stay calm and balanced when you are avid about something. Wearing, meditating on, or surrounding yourself with Henna helps you stay flexible and open to new possibilities.

Compatible birthdays:
January 3 • August 8 • October 28

Henna = PANTONE 19-1334

WITHERED ROSE

INFLUENTIAL
PERSISTENT
CURIOUS

If you were born on this day:
People gravitate to your natural magnetism. You have a certain way of seeing things and want to be treated with respect. You are sometimes torn between the practical side of life and the creative and imaginative side. Although you may see yourself as logical, you are far more emotional than even you may realize.

How this color benefits you:
Your personal color helps ease the conflicting parts of your nature. Wearing, meditating on, or surrounding yourself with Withered Rose teaches you to honor the unique and special parts of yourself and others.

Compatible birthdays:
July 5 • October 30 • December 9

Withered Rose = PANTONE 18-1435

APRICOT TAN

PERSUASIVE
LEADER
CHARISMATIC

If you were born on this day:
You are a born leader and a great communicator. You have a lot of energy and like to think for yourself. It is important that you connect your energy with spiritual intention, or you may lose track of what is truly important. It is your affinity with the spiritual that will keep you focused.

How this color benefits you:
Your personal color helps you direct your sensitivity. Wearing, meditating on, or surrounding yourself with Apricot Tan can help you remain humble as you demonstrate different leadership roles.

Compatible birthdays:
April 10 • September 10 • December 3

Apricot Tan = PANTONE 15-1237

SMOKE GREEN

INTELLIGENT
EMOTIONAL
INTENSE

If you were born on this day:
You are highly intelligent and love to learn. Your mind is able to grasp ideas and concepts easily. You can be generous and inspirational to those you come in contact with. Your challenge lies in the emotional area of your life. When you have been hurt or disappointed, interacting with others becomes more difficult, and you can lose your normal trust in humanity.

How this color benefits you:
Your personal color vibrates with financial ease and freedom. Wearing, meditating on, or surrounding yourself with Smoke Green reminds you to let go of the past and stay in the present, where miracles can occur.

Compatible birthdays:
February 3 • May 18 • July 15

Smoke Green = PANTONE 15-6315

MANDARIN ORANGE

MUSICAL
VERBAL
TENACIOUS

If you were born on this day:
Youthful and friendly, you love to talk and interact with others. Many people born on this day have a gift for writing or public speaking. You like to be on the move. You do need to practice flexibility as you move toward your goals. Tenacity and agility combined with work and play will ensure success.

How this color benefits you:
Your personal color helps you make the most of every moment. Wearing, meditating on, or surrounding yourself with Mandarin Orange reminds you to take action and not get caught up in the world of ideas.

Compatible birthdays:
January 31 • February 26 • October 1

Mandarin Orange = PANTONE 16-1459

PERIDOT

DRAMATIC
POISED
KNOWLEDGEABLE

If you were born on this day:
You are extremely intelligent and love to learn. Being productive is important to you. You need to move physically toward your dreams and not get stuck in fear or confusion. Your answers come to you through faith and action.

How this color benefits you:
Your personal color helps ease any worry you may be carrying. Wearing, meditating on, or surrounding yourself with Peridot helps ease financial pressures and connects you to the spiritual side of your nature and your true calling.

Compatible birthdays:
March 27 • October 11 • November 9

Peridot = PANTONE 17-0336

HOLLY GREEN

ORIGINAL
VERBALLY GIFTED
PLAYFUL

If you were born on this day:
Some of the greatest, most giving people were born on this day. Your natural desire to help anyone at any time is unparalleled. Your talent with words makes you a natural at writing, speaking, and storytelling. You are good at so many things, you may find yourself scattering your energies.

How this color benefits you:
Your personal color resonates with physical vitality. Wearing, meditating on, or surrounding yourself with Holly Green replenishes your enthusiasm and stamina so that you can continue to touch people's lives and inspire others.

Compatible birthdays:
March 14 • April 10 • June 26

Holly Green = PANTONE 16-5932

SEEDLING

MENTALLY AGILE
ANALYTICAL
SENSITIVE

If you were born on this day:
You carry a wealth of information and love to learn. Your thirst for knowledge is ravenous, and your mind usually works overtime. You have a sensitive and emotional side that is hidden under an array of facts and figures. It is important that you find a balance between the analytical side of yourself and the side that nurtures spiritual awareness.

How this color benefits you:
Your personal color encourages trust and self-confidence. Wearing, meditating on, or surrounding your-self with Seedling promotes ease as you develop a strong sense of responsibility.

Compatible birthdays:
February 14 • April 14 • September 14

Seedling = PANTONE 14-0217

NILE GREEN

MUSICAL
VERBAL
TRAVELER

If you were born on this day:
You are highly verbal and not afraid to speak your mind. Many people born on this day have a talent for music and writing. You have a strong private side and are not always emotionally available. It is sometimes difficult for you to share your personal feelings in intimate relationships.

How this color benefits you:
Your personal color can help you experience a constant flow of joy in your life. Wearing, meditating on, or surrounding yourself with Nile Green helps rid the body of doubt, criticism, and judgment.

Compatible birthdays:
June 30 • November 7 • December 12

Nile Green = PANTONE 14-0121

PEACH BEIGE

SPIRITUAL
GENEROUS
PENETRATING

If you were born on this day:
You are spiritually driven and relentless in your quest for transformation and enlightenment. You hold yourself to a higher authority. Simple societal laws and rules do not always work for you. You can be generous to a fault because you are deeply aware that we are all connected.

How this color benefits you:
Your personal color helps you stay balanced as you move through challenging experiences. Wearing, meditating on, or surrounding yourself with Peach Beige enables you to carry your message of love and grace to others without draining your own vital energy.

Compatible birthdays:
March 31 • June 13 • November 17

Peach Beige = PANTONE 15-1516

DILL

FRIENDLY
OUTDOORSY
DEVOTED

If you were born on this day:
You have a natural charm that people enjoy. Communicating with others is an important part of your evolution. Your talents are many, and you can usually excel in quite a few fields. Try not to isolate yourself from others.

How this color benefits you:
Your personal color helps you blend the introverted and extroverted parts of your nature. Wearing, meditating on,or surrounding yourself with Dill infuses courage and calls in like-minded individuals with whom you can share your experiences.

Compatible birthdays:
March 23 • April 27 • August 18

Dill = PANTONE 18-0108

BUTTERSCOTCH

FEISTY
LEADER
ENERGETIC

If you were born on this day:
You have strong convictions and are able to lead others. You can be feisty and are not afraid to speak your mind. Goal-oriented, you like to set your sights on something and work steadily toward it. There is a sensitive side to your nature that not everyone can see. It is important to channel this sensitivity to avoid becoming irritable or defensive.

How this color benefits you:
Your personal color helps you listen to others with empathy while moving toward your own goals. Wearing, meditating on, or surrounding yourself with Butterscotch keeps you calm, focused, and able to include others on your journey.

Compatible birthdays:
August 6 • September 19 • October 14

Butterscotch = PANTONE 15-1147

PASTEL LILAC

PARTNER ORIENTED
STYLISH
FUNNY

If you were born on this day:
Many people born on this day know the value of being in a relationship. Whether it is a romantic, business, or any other type of association, you are a wonderful partner and ally. Finding balance is the main challenge for you. You have a great sense of style and a casual ease that people just adore.

How this color benefits you:
Your personal color helps you listen to your body and your inner voice. Wearing, meditating on, or surrounding yourself with Pastel Lilac gives you the courage to take care of yourself first, so that you have the energy to be the wonderful person and partner you want to become.

Compatible birthdays:
January 31 • April 14 • June 16

Pastel Lilac = PANTONE 14-3812

BURNT ORANGE

COLORFUL
UNIQUE
COMMUNICATOR

If you were born on this day:
Action could be your middle name.
You are never boring, and your life
usually moves rapidly. Your mind is
quick and quirky. You can do more
in a week than most people can do
in a month. Scattering your energy
in too many directions is often a
problem. It is important that you
care for your body and learn how
to stay in the present.

How this color benefits you:
Your personal color reminds you to
embrace each moment. Wearing,
meditating on, or surrounding yourself with Burnt Orange encourages
loyalty, moderation, and relaxation.

Compatible birthdays:
May 4 • June 30 • August 14

Burnt Orange = PANTONE 16-1448

GRASSHOPPER

ENDURING
ACTIVE
INTELLIGENT

If you were born on this day:
You are smart and witty and know how to communicate. You are good at a variety of things and can be found doing more than one job at once. Life for you is an adventure. A good relationship is important to your well-being, and you function best when you have someone with whom to share your experiences. You are often interested in the spiritual and soulful side of life.

How this color benefits you:
Your personal color can keep you grounded as you move through changes in your life. Wearing, meditating on, or surrounding yourself with Grasshopper helps you process information and manage your responsibilities.

Compatible birthdays:
March 4 • April 13 • November 13

Grasshopper = PANTONE 18-0332

JUNE

ASPEN GOLD

RADIANT
INTELLECTUALLY ENERGIZING
UPLIFTING

The color for the month of June is Aspen Gold. Energizing and activating, this is a color filled with radiance and light. Aspen Gold has the ability to lift our spirits and bring sunshine into our lives. Mercury, the planet of communication, moves through the heavens during the month of June. Yellow is known for stimulating the brain and increasing intelligence and mental agility.

Aspen Gold = PANTONE 13-0850

JUNE

ASPEN GOLD can be used by anyone to increase communication and memory skills.

Aspen Gold is similar to sunshine. Its color rays dispel darkness while increasing joy and optimism. Wearing it can enhance articulation and verbal dexterity—words seem to flow easily when this color is in view. It can be especially useful when taking an exam or speaking in front of an audience.

DAFFODIL

GENEROUS SPIRITUAL ENTERTAINER

If you were born on this day:
Some of the kindest and most generous people were born on this day. You have an unusual mixture of inner tenderness and extroverted star quality. Balancing both sides of your nature will keep you busy as you try to maintain a foothold on your integrity and express your talents to the world.

How this color benefits you:
Your personal color reminds you that by honoring yourself, you will honor others as well. Wearing, meditating on, or surrounding yourself with Daffodil can renew your energy when you are feeling lost or depleted. It reminds you of the light and enthusiasm that you have within.

Compatible birthdays:
March 19 • April 8 • July 23

Daffodil = PANTONE 14-0850

NILE

NEGOTIATOR
CLEVER
LIVELY

If you were born on this day:
You are naturally playful and fun to be with. You enjoy relationships but can get bored easily. You tend to juggle and can often be found doing two things at once. You are good at interacting with others and organizing deals. You have an ambitious side that requires you to be both practical and persistent.

How this color benefits you:
Your personal color helps blend the charismatic side of your personality with fearlessness and determination. Wearing, meditating on, or surroun- ding yourself with Nile helps you attract a partner who matches your vibration. It moves you away from juggling and gives you the courage to choose.

Compatible birthdays:
January 25 • August 27 • November 22

Nile = PANTONE 14-0223

PUMPKIN

ENDEARING
PLAYFUL
QUICK-WITTED

If you were born on this day:
People find you endearing and enjoyable. You can often be found in the entertainment business because of your wit and sensuality. You have a personal side that you do not share with everyone. Extremely bright, you can feel separate and misunderstood when people don't appreciate your thought process.

How this color benefits you:
Your personal color inspires you to express your total self and not just a limited persona. Wearing, meditating on, or surrounding yourself with Pumpkin helps you integrate the emotional with the intellectual side of your nature.

Compatible birthdays:
January 20 • March 21 • October 8

Pumpkin = PANTONE 14-1139

GREEN GLOW

HARDWORKING
ENTERPRISING
TENACIOUS

If you were born on this day:
You are hardworking and quick to discover opportunities. Achievement is important to you, and you are not afraid to work long and hard to reach your destination. You are mentally alert and can easily grasp ideas and concepts. It is important for you to embrace the flexible and humanitarian side of your nature.

How this color benefits you:
Your personal color helps you know when to shine and when to share. Wearing, meditating on, or surrounding yourself with Green Glow promotes belief and compassion. It also encourages you to interact with others on a more intimate level.

Compatible birthdays:
April 20 • November 10 • December 30

Green Glow = PANTONE 13-0442

MING

EXUBERANT
FRIENDLY
YOUTHFUL

If you were born on this day:
Life is not boring when you are around. Your energy is high, and you love to have a good time. You are aware that life can be magical, and you are ready for the adventure. You have a strong spiritual calling and desire to do something special and meaningful with your life.

How this color benefits you:
Your personal color helps you slow down so that you can receive the answers that only come when you are in a restful place. Wearing, meditating on, or surrounding yourself with Ming helps you release excess energy and become quietly conscious.

Compatible birthdays:
April 11 • July 23 • October 23

Ming = PANTONE 15-6120

CORAL REEF

INSTINCTIVE
INDEPENDENT
SOCIAL

If you were born on this day:
You have a sensual and convincing nature. Once you commit to something, you like to go all the way. Although you are independent and enjoy traveling, a home base to return to is important for you. A strong family and a solid foundation give you the support necessary to accomplish your dreams.

How this color benefits you:
Your personal color integrates the quality of discipline with desire. Wearing, meditating on, or surrounding yourself with Coral Reef helps you ride through life with care, consciousness, and childlike wonder.

Compatible birthdays:
January 15 • May 10 • November 28

Coral Reef = PANTONE 15-1331

JUNE 07

VIOLET ICE

SEDUCTIVE
MUSICAL
INSPIRING

If you were born on this day:
People look to you for inspiration.
You are one of a kind and not afraid
to be different. Your talent comes
from a deep and powerful place.
You were born to communicate,
so it is important that you are conscious of what you say and do.
You have an innate talent for
building your dreams and can
do well financially.

How this color benefits you:
Your personal color resonates with
spirituality. Wearing, meditating on,
or surrounding yourself with Violet
Ice helps you maintain balance as
you share your life with others.

Compatible birthdays:
February 8 • August 15 •
November 23

Violet Ice = PANTONE 15-2706

GOLDEN APRICOT

INFLUENTIAL
METHODICAL
LIVELY

If you were born on this day:
You notice opportunity and are always ready for something new and exciting. You are quick on your feet, and people naturally like you. You are usually found with a smile on your face, no matter how hard you are working. Many people born on this day have a way with finances.

How this color benefits you:
Your personal color helps ground your aspirations. Wearing, meditating on, or surrounding yourself with Golden Apricot reminds you to keep things fresh and not get stuck in old ideas, habits, or relationships.

Compatible birthdays:
February 17 • November 17 • December 21

Golden Apricot = PANTONE 14-1041

AMBERLIGHT

DRAMATIC
CREATIVE
SENSITIVE

If you were born on this day:
You are enormously creative and inspiring to watch and be around. You have your own way of thinking and doing things. You come across as self-assured and powerful. You tend to have a strong point of view, so it is important to cultivate flexibility and ease when dealing with others.

How this color benefits you:
Your personal color blends greatness with humility. Wearing, meditating on, or surrounding yourself with Amberlight helps you know when to plow through and when to bend.

Compatible birthdays:
January 17 • March 27 • October 10

Amberlight = PANTONE 14-1217

GOLDEN NUGGET

INTENT
SMART
SUCCESSFUL

JUNE 10

If you were born on this day:
You were born for success, and you enjoy the limelight. Smart and capable, you don't like to wait for anyone else to give you permission to do something. You are intellectually active, and your mind works overtime. Physical activity is important for your well-being.

How this color benefits you:
Your personal color intensifies your shining spirit. Wearing, meditating on, or surrounding yourself with Golden Nugget helps you balance your emotions and keep your mood on an even keel.

Compatible birthdays:
January 19 • April 16 • July 7

Golden Nugget = PANTONE 16-1142

SUNSET GOLD

INTUITIVE
ARTICULATE
FUNNY

If you were born on this day:
You were born with a nice combination of strength and sensitivity. You function best when you have a partner or a good friend to share your adventures with. Your depth of understanding makes you easy to talk to. The challenges that occur in your life serve to uncover your innate strengths, which may lie dormant if not for those experiences.

How this color benefits you:
Wearing, meditating on, or surrounding yourself with Sunset Gold helps increase your self-discipline and transform hurts and setbacks into knowledge and opportunities.

Compatible birthdays:
February 7 • April 17 • October 5

Sunset Gold = PANTONE 13-0940

BIRD OF PARADISE

WRITER
SELF-SUFFICIENT
STORYTELLER

JUNE 12

If you were born on this day:
You have a way with words and know how to tell a story. Whether you are writing or speaking, you are able to convey human emotion through your nuances and expressions. You are capable of motivating and influencing others, so it is important to ask for higher guidance to stay on the right path.

How this color benefits you:
Your personal color helps connect you to your soul's purpose. Wearing, meditating on, or surrounding yourself with Bird of Paradise helps you discover the common thread between responsibility and freedom.

Compatible birthdays:
February 18 • April 14 • July 22

Bird of Paradise = PANTONE 16-1357

BRIGHT CHARTREUSE

CREATIVE
LOVING
CAPABLE

If you were born on this day:
Your creative talents are numerous.
Capable and *kind* are just some of
the words that best describe you.
Whether you write, draw, perform,
or fight for human rights, you are
often called upon to step up to the
plate, even though you have a shy
streak. You can see what you are
really made of when confronted
with a crisis or challenge.

How this color benefits you:
Your personal color helps you
resonate with strength and vitality.
Wearing, meditating on, or
surrounding yourself with Bright
Chartreuse invokes financial
protection and trust in the universe.

Compatible birthdays:
April 5 • July 4 • November 26

Bright Chartreuse = PANTONE 14-0445

SPRING BOUQUET

CLEVER
CHARMING
CHILDLIKE

If you were born on this day:
Life is an adventure that you want to enjoy. Your mind is alert, and you know how to act quickly. Social and charming, you are someone people like to have around. Your childlike quality is especially disarming, and people are often unaware of the part of you that is strong and ambitious.

How this color benefits you:
Your personal color helps calm your nervous system. Wearing, meditating on, or surrounding yourself with Spring Bouquet increases ease and harmony in your environment and helps you connect more intimately with others.

Compatible birthdays:
March 31 • July 24 • December 26

Spring Bouquet = PANTONE 14-6340

APRICOT NECTAR

STRIKING
PLEASANT
APPEALING

If you were born on this day:
You are easy to get along with, and people gravitate to you. You are naturally generous and love to talk and communicate with others. You have an instinctive attraction to beauty and art and gravitate toward luxury items. Your sensual nature enjoys life and all of its pleasures.

How this color benefits you:
Your personal color highlights your perceptive abilities. Wearing, meditating on, or surrounding yourself with Apricot Nectar helps calm your mental restlessness. It grounds your energy without diluting your fresh and joyous spirit.

Compatible birthdays:
February 11 • April 7 • August 22

Apricot Nectar = PANTONE 14-1133

RAFFIA

QUICK
WITTY
STRIVING

If you were born on this day:
You have the ability to achieve your aims when striving for financial success or a social cause. You are quick and witty and can easily move in and out of circles and situations. You want to be free to express yourself. Although it is important for you to have some structure in your life, you don't enjoy restrictions or a job that is too dull or predictable.

How this color benefits you:
Your personal color emphasizes the intuitive and spiritual side of life. Wearing, meditating on, or surrounding yourself with Raffia helps you see the true value of things.

Compatible birthdays:
April 9 • September 7 • October 6

Raffia = PANTONE 13-0725

CANYON SUNSET

CHARISMATIC
POWERFUL
SOCIAL

If you were born on this day:
People are naturally drawn to your energy and charisma. Interacting with others stimulates you and makes you feel alive. You are persuasive and can be aggressive if needed. You can instigate change and enthusiasm when you are present. Quick on your feet, you are not easy to control or manipulate.

How this color benefits you:
Your personal color helps ground your energy so you can carve your own unique path. Wearing, meditating on, or surrounding yourself with Canyon Sunset gives you the energy to move beyond obstacles or challenges.

Compatible birthdays:
May 8 • August 15 • October 31

Canyon Sunset = PANTONE 15-1333

BRANDIED MELON

INTERESTING
DURABLE
EFFECTIVE

JUNE 18

If you were born on this day:
You have style and class. No matter what you do, you are recognized as being special in some way. You have a rare combination of strength, depth, and compassion. You have a royal quality that can make you feel a little separate at times.

How this color benefits you:
Your personal color connects you to your inner strength. Wearing, meditating on, or surrounding yourself with Brandied Melon enhances your intuitive nature and allows you to pull in people who are on a similar life path.

Compatible birthdays:
April 8 • May 27 • October 20

Brandied Melon = PANTONE 16-1340

GOLDEN OCHRE

LIVELY
VERBAL
TENACIOUS

If you were born on this day:
You have a natural brilliance and are usually a step ahead of everyone else. Your mind is quick and alert. You have a youthful quality, and even when you are older, you will always have a twinkle in your eye that belies your age. It can be difficult for you to relax.

How this color benefits you:
Your personal color supports your authentic self. Wearing, meditating on, or surrounding yourself with Golden Ochre helps calm your nervous system by integrating your emotions and focusing your energy.

Compatible birthdays:
May 23 • October 27 • November 25

Golden Ochre = PANTONE 16-1346

LETTUCE GREEN

IMAGINATIVE
EMOTIONAL
DISCRIMINATING

If you were born on this day:
You have strong emotions but do not always express what you are really feeling. You have a way with words and are mentally agile. Partnerships are important to you, and a lot of transformation occurs due to your close personal relationships. Writing is one of the ways for you to process your feelings and channel your energy.

How this color benefits you:
Your personal color helps increase your stamina. Wearing, meditating on, or surrounding yourself with Lettuce Green lets you know when to rest and when to act.

Compatible birthdays:
March 3 • April 26 • October 14

Lettuce Green = PANTONE 13-0324

CHAMOIS

PASSIONATE
WARM
MONEYMAKER

If you were born on this day:
Many people born on this day have a great deal of sensuality. You have a good imagination, and when you focus your energy, you have a talent for making your dreams come true. It is important not to dissipate your energy by just thinking about what you want. When you have an idea, be sure to take an action toward your desired goal, no matter how small it may seem.

How this color benefits you:
Your personal color resonates with confidence and courage. Wearing, meditating on, or surrounding yourself with Chamois helps you share your gifts and talents with others.

Compatible birthdays:
April 3 • August 16 • December 23

Chamois = PANTONE 15-1145

BRIGHT LIME GREEN

INVENTIVE
THEATRICAL
EARNEST

JUNE 22

If you were born on this day:
You have a strong inner world that is rich with imagination. You have the ability to build your dreams into a solid and fortuitous reality. Although you can be practical, you also have a strong, feeling nature. Therefore, it is important for you to express your creativity and innovative ideas.

How this color benefits you:
Your personal color helps you relate to others with ease. Wearing, meditating on, or surrounding yourself with Bright Lime Green increases your adaptability and helps stabilize your emotions.

Compatible birthdays:
February 28 • April 4 • June 27

Bright Lime Green = PANTONE 14-0244

JUNE 23

BRIGHT AQUA

GENTLE
STRONG
CREATIVE

If you were born on this day:
You are enormously creative and capable of making things happen. You know how to make magic if you do not let your emotions overwhelm you. You need encouragement and supportive friends and allies.

How this color benefits you:
Your personal color gives you breadth of vision. Wearing, meditating on, or surrounding yourself with Bright Aqua disperses self-doubt and increases your vitality and sense of self.

Compatible birthdays:
August 7 • August 21 • November 1

Bright Aqua = PANTONE 16-5422

TIGERLILY

COMMUNICATOR
INSIGHTFUL
MYSTICAL

If you were born on this day:
Your ability to affect people is powerful. Highly intelligent, you enjoy learning and sharing information and concepts. You are discriminating and can cut to the truth and convey ideas with insight and assurance. You are highly magnetic and can change the world with your intention, poise, and charisma.

How this color benefits you:
Your personal color resonates with love. Wearing, meditating on, or surrounding yourself with Tigerlily uplifts your spirit and helps you stay connected to the truth and your special mission in life.

Compatible birthdays:
January 10 • March 4 • July 6

Tigerlily = PANTONE 17-1456

GULL GRAY

RECEPTIVE
LOYAL
INSIGHTFUL

If you were born on this day:
You have the ability to touch people
deeply. Whether through your healing hands or your unusual way with
words, your special something has
a way of changing people's lives.
You are loyal to your principles and
to the people you love.

How this color benefits you:
Your personal color helps balance
your emotions. Wearing, meditating
on, or surrounding yourself with Gull
Gray helps you connect with others
without losing your own spiritual
way.

Compatible birthdays:
August 17 • October 8 •
December 28

Gull Gray = PANTONE 16-3803

RAW SIENNA

FEISTY
NURTURING
ADVENTUROUS

If you were born on this day:
It is important for you to remain active and connected to nature. You need to have a way to express your feelings and release pent-up stress. Try not to get bogged down by monetary worries. Many of your challenges can be triggers for opportunity. You need to see what you are made of by pushing yourself out of your comfort zone and into the world of adventure.

How this color benefits you:
Your personal color resonates with strength and will. Wearing, meditating on, or surrounding yourself with Raw Sienna increases your resilience and helps dissolve old wounds.

Compatible birthdays:
April 29 • May 27 • November 17

Raw Sienna = PANTONE 17-1436

CRABAPPLE

BRILLIANT
ENCOURAGING
DIFFERENT

If you were born on this day:
You are not the run-of-the-mill type, and you want to make a difference. You have a lot of energy and power, and many do very well in sports. Highly intelligent, your mind is constantly learning and acquiring information.

How this color benefits you:
Your personal color resonates with emotional understanding. Wearing, meditating on, or surrounding yourself with Crabapple urges you to act. It encourages you to move through life with trust and commitment.

Compatible birthdays:
September 12 • November 16 • December 12

Crabapple = PANTONE 16-1532

ORANGE OCHRE

INTELLIGENT
SOPHISTICATED
AMBITIOUS

If you were born on this day:
You have the ability to lead and inspire others just by being true to yourself. Your natural grace and dignity enable you to resonate with the higher stratospheres of life. You are independent and keep a lot of your personal thoughts and feelings to yourself. Being selective, you are able to choose your associates wisely.

How this color benefits you:
Your personal color resonates with sunshine. Wearing, meditating on, or surrounding yourself with Orange Ochre inspires optimism and joy and dissolves any illusion of separateness you may feel.

Compatible birthdays:
November 22 • November 28 • December 22

Orange Ochre = PANTONE 16-1253

FOREST SHADE

EMOTIONAL
QUICK
PRIVATE

If you were born on this day:
Quick and articulate, you are known for your sense of humor. Friends enjoy your company and miss you when you are not around. You keep a lot of what you feel to yourself and enjoy a private life that few people will ever see. A loving home and family are very important to you.

How this color benefits you:
Your personal color resonates with peace and assurance. Wearing, meditating on, or surrounding yourself with Forest Shade promotes growth and helps you let go of old ideas and patterns.

Compatible birthdays:
January 22 • April 16 • November 20

Forest Shade = PANTONE 15-6423

CADMIUM ORANGE

ROMANTIC
DESIRABLE
DRAMATIC

JUNE 30

If you were born on this day:
Love is very important to you, and you can be extremely devoted to your mate, family, friends, or profession. Once you put your mind to something, you tend to go all the way. You have a regal manner and like attention and devotion. It is essential that you are treated with respect.

How this color benefits you:
Your personal color encourages a healthy and flexible outlook on life. Wearing, meditating on, or surrounding yourself with Cadmium Orange helps you move forward with vision and freedom.

Compatible birthdays:
March 2 • August 25 • December 30

Cadmium Orange = PANTONE 15-1340

JULY

CORAL BLUSH

SOOTHING
RECEPTIVE
NURTURING

The color for the month of July is
Coral Blush. Gentle and soothing,
Coral Blush inspires love and
receptivity. The moon rules the
skies during the month of July, and
just as the moon goes through its
phases and cycles, so do we. The
silver in this color signifies the value
of change, reflection, and receptivity, and the pink represents love and
tenderness. Together, they make a
color that can be used in times of
change or transition and as an aid
for emotional healing.

Coral Blush = PANTONE 14-1909

CORAL BLUSH can be used by anyone to open the heart and lift the spirit.

JULY

Coral Blush aligns with feminine energy and increases receptivity. It helps attract love and sweetness into your life. This color can help you receive love and care from others and can be very useful when moving through family traumas. Coral Blush can help you adjust to changes and carry you peacefully through the cycles of life.

PALE BLUSH

KIND
COMPASSIONATE
HIDDEN

If you were born on this day:
You were born with a perfect blend of strength and gentleness. Your ability to read people and to show acts of kindness comes quite naturally to you. Perceptive and sensitive, you are able to pick up subtle cues and nuances. You are highly emotional and long for people to understand you as well as you understand them.

How this color benefits you:
Your personal color promotes self-confidence and emotional stability. Wearing, meditating on, or surrounding yourself with Pale Blush helps you move in and out of your private and public lives with ease.

Compatible birthdays:
January 7 • May 16 • September 7

Pale Blush = PANTONE 14-1312

FRAGRANT LILAC

ARTISTIC
PARTNER-ORIENTED
INDEPENDENT

JULY 02

If you were born on this day:
Most people born on this day are artistic and imaginative. You also have the ability to be quite logical and are often able to merge your special talents into lucrative endeavors. You have a strong spiritual calling, and the people and circumstances you encounter serve to move you closer to an enlightened state of being.

How this color benefits you:
Your personal color encourages you to believe in yourself. Wearing, meditating on, or surrounding your-self with Fragrant Lilac helps ease monetary concerns and reduces friction within relationships.

Compatible birthdays:
June 20 • September 9 • November 9

Fragrant Lilac = PANTONE 14-3204

SHELL CORAL

FRIENDLY
OPTIMISTIC
ASPIRING

If you were born on this day:
People tend to gravitate toward you. You have a truthful and cordial manner that increases your popularity. You are ambitious and aspire to reach great heights. A natural communicator, you have the ability to easily move in and out of different social circles. Although you can appear outgoing, you keep your private thoughts and feelings hidden.

How this color benefits you:
Your personal color protects your spirit. Wearing, meditating on, or surrounding yourself with Shell Coral allows you to move through the world with grace and security.

Compatible birthdays:
May 12 • August 25 • November 28

Shell Coral = PANTONE 15-1334

LILY GREEN

BUILDER
HOME-ORIENTED
EMOTIONAL

If you were born on this day:
A loving home and family are important to your emotional well-being. You are a natural builder, and creating a strong foundation on which to build is imperative. You are not afraid to work hard to achieve your aims. Productivity and financial security are things that you take very seriously.

How this color benefits you:
Your personal color helps balance responsibility with playfulness. Wearing, meditating on, or surrounding yourself with Lily Green reminds you to share your gifts and talents within your community and with the world at large.

Compatible birthdays:
January 20 • April 22 • December 4

Lily Green = PANTONE 13-0317

AQUATIC

INTERESTING
FUNNY
COMMITTED

If you were born on this day:
You have a great sense of humor, and people love to laugh when you are near them. You have a unique way of seeing things. You are innovative and interesting and, when confident, are extremely creative and resourceful. Try not to let doubt or conflicting emotions impede your productivity and growth.

How this color benefits you:
Your personal color enhances your appealing nature. Wearing, meditating on, or surrounding yourself with Aquatic protects you from debilitating emotions while allowing you to receive the good fortunes that await you.

Compatible birthdays:
January 5 • April 5 • July 3

Aquatic = PANTONE 14-4510

FAIR ORCHID

GENEROUS
ORGANIZED
RESPONSIBLE

If you were born on this day:
Although you are highly sensitive, you know how to get the job done. You have learned how to move around your emotional nature to ensure a life of productivity and stability. You are creative and organized and are usually able to integrate these two qualities. People come to you for advice and support because of your generous and nurturing spirit.

How this color benefits you:
Your personal color resonates with detachment and vision. Wearing, meditating on, or surrounding yourself with Fair Orchid brings harmony to the mind, body, and spirit.

Compatible birthdays:
January 14 • September 24 • December 13

Fair Orchid = PANTONE 15-3508

PERSIAN JEWEL

INTELLIGENT
SEDUCTIVE
SENSITIVE

If you were born on this day:
You have a great sense of humor and know how to read people and situations with profound accuracy. You are highly emotional and sensitive and so may have developed a strong protective layer. It is not easy for others to permeate that shield, even though connecting on a deep level is your heart's desire. You are sensual, and people find you extremely seductive.

How this color benefits you:
Your personal color helps release emotional wounds and protective patterns that no longer serve you. Wearing, meditating on, or surrounding yourself with Persian Jewel helps you stay in the moment, where new life continually unfolds.

Compatible birthdays:
March 14 • July 16 • August 25

Persian Jewel = PANTONE 17-3934

LILAC MARBLE

WILLFUL
POWERFUL
CAUTIOUS

If you were born on this day:
You have a strong independent streak, and with proper support, you are unstoppable. You are sometimes your own worst enemy because it is not easy for you to ask for help. Try not to isolate yourself from others. You have a great amount of courage and stamina, so don't let negative emotions drain your energy.

How this color benefits you:
Your personal color gives you the courage to trust without losing your sense of self. Wearing, meditating on, or surrounding yourself with Lilac Marble keeps you light-hearted and confident that you can achieve your goals.

Compatible birthdays:
July 24 • August 15 • October 15

Lilac Marble = PANTONE 14-3903

SILVER PINK

THEATRICAL
SENSITIVE
RESOURCEFUL

If you were born on this day:
You have a range of talents from which to choose. Your perception and ability to size up a situation or opportunity is quite remarkable. Strong yet sensitive, you are not always as confident as you may seem. Frequent rest periods are needed for you to relax and rejuvenate. Finding your place in the world and having a balanced home life are your challenges.

How this color benefits you:
Your personal color inspires confidence and enchantment. Wearing, meditating on, or surrounding yourself with Silver Pink connects you with the magical and miraculous side of life.

Compatible birthdays:
May 14 • August 19 • December 18

Silver Pink = PANTONE 14-1508

APRICOT ICE

INDEPENDENT
FEISTY
TENACIOUS

If you were born on this day:
People turn their heads when you walk into a room. You have star quality and know how to shine and look the part. People come to you when they want to get the job done. Many people born on this day are leaders and have executive abilities. You have an independent streak and do not take kindly to people telling you what to do.

How this color benefits you:
Your personal color eases your protective persona and inspires your true radiance. Wearing, meditating on, or surrounding yourself with Apricot Ice increases your open and loving nature.

Compatible birthdays:
January 6 • May 26 • December 14

Apricot Ice = PANTONE 13-1020

POTPOURRI

AMBITIOUS
SMART
STYLISH

If you were born on this day:
People born on this day have a natural sense of style. Although you have a strong feeling nature, you are able to push your emotions aside in order to do things you have to do. You choose to keep going when most people give up.

How this color benefits you:
Your personal color helps balance some of the ambiguity you have within. Wearing, meditating on, or surrounding yourself with Potpourri inspires trust in relationships. It integrates strength with sensitivity and independence with desire, enabling you to share true love.

Compatible birthdays:
April 5 • August 10 • October 17

Potpourri = PANTONE 13-2004

PEACH PINK

DELIGHTFUL
ENTERTAINING
PROFOUND

If you were born on this day:
People adore you and find you irresistible. You were born with a tremendous amount of charm and magnetism. You have a giving nature and will go to great lengths to be a valued friend. You are a sensitive spirit and want to be treated with respect and kindness.

How this color benefits you:
Your personal color embodies the qualities of courage, youth, and vitality. Wearing, meditating on, or surrounding yourself with Peach Pink helps you move through life with trust, optimism, and assertion.

Compatible birthdays:
January 12 • June 25 • November 26

Peach Pink = PANTONE 15-1530

SEAFOAM GREEN

CAPABLE
ENTERPRISING
TALENTED

If you were born on this day:
Many people born on this day are enterprising and want to build their careers. Practical and creative, you have the ability to start something from scratch and make it grow. You are independent but also enjoy being in a relationship. Try not to get too serious or let your emotions weigh too heavily on your heart.

How this color benefits you:
Your personal color helps ease any monetary concerns you may have. Wearing, meditating on, or surrounding yourself with Seafoam Green encourages action, joy, and participation with others.

Compatible birthdays:
February 12 • August 20 • October 26

Seafoam Green = PANTONE 12-0313

DELPHINIUM BLUE

COMMUNICATOR
EXPRESSIVE
ENDURING

If you were born on this day:
The need to express yourself is inherent to your personality. Any form of creative release helps balance your mental, physical, and emotional well-being. You are kind-hearted and not afraid to offer insights and words of support to people you meet. The desire for love is very important to you.

How this color benefits you:
Your personal color inspires breadth of scope. Wearing, meditating on, or surrounding yourself with Delphinium Blue invokes trust and ease in regard to love and finances.

Compatible birthdays:
January 5 • August 21 • November 30

Delphinium Blue = PANTONE 16-4519

MOONLITE MAUVE

CURIOUS
INTELLIGENT
IMPRESSIVE

If you were born on this day:
Many people born on this day are great coordinators. You have an ability to gather information and relay it to others. You take your work seriously, and therefore people find you impressive. You are able to attract good fortune, especially with regard to finances. Connecting with the spiritual side of life and doing something that contributes to society bring you peace and happiness.

How this color benefits you:
Your personal color inspires trust in the universal plan. Wearing, meditating on, or surrounding yourself with Moonlite Mauve balances the playful with the serious side of your nature.

Compatible birthdays:
January 8 • September 13 • November 20

Moonlite Mauve = PANTONE 16-2614

BRANDIED APRICOT

MUSICAL
SPUNKY
APPEALING

If you were born on this day:
Because of your passionate nature, you have the ability to influence others. You have an appealing personality, and people want to be near you. Your strong will and focus help you climb to great heights. You are inventive and inspirational.

How this color benefits you:
Your personal color resonates with the humanitarian side of life. Wearing, meditating on, or surrounding yourself with Brandied Apricot helps you confront change and difficulties. It increases your tolerance and connects you to the source of your wisdom.

Compatible birthdays:
March 10 • August 5 • September 20

Brandied Apricot = PANTONE 16-1610

IRIS

INTERESTING
PRIVATE
PROVOCATIVE

If you were born on this day:
There is always something unusual and provocative about people born on this day. You are your own person, and you like to do things in your own way. You are not the type to follow others. You can be seductive and controlling when you want to be.

How this color benefits you:
Your personal color helps you connect with others while dissolving feelings of isolation. Wearing, meditating on, or surrounding yourself with Iris allows ease and flexibility as you move through obstacles.

Compatible birthdays:
February 18 • October 12 • November 24

Iris = PANTONE 14-3805

TERRA COTTA
COMMITTED
EXPLORER
ANALYTICAL

If you were born on this day:
You have a strong and dynamic personality. You have a great ability to think and analyze problems and situations. Although you can be highly emotional, it is your mind that works overtime. Once you commit to something, you tend to be in it for the long haul.

How this color benefits you:
Your personal color inspires the soulful and spiritual side of your nature. Wearing, meditating on, or surrounding yourself with Terra Cotta heightens your belief in love and miracles.

Compatible birthdays:
January 19 • August 28 • December 24

Terra Cotta = PANTONE 16-1526

TANGERINE

INQUISITIVE
TALENTED
INDEPENDENT

If you were born on this day:
You are constantly learning and exploring life and all of its wonders. Whether you are an artist or an analyst, you delve deeply into whatever it is that captures your interest. Although you are social and need to interact with others, you have a very strong autonomous side.

How this color benefits you:
Your personal color helps you integrate the outgoing with the introverted side of your nature. Wearing, meditating on, or surrounding yourself with Tangerine increases clarity and receptivity.

Compatible birthdays:
January 18 • May 8 • August 24

Tangerine = PANTONE 15-1247

BUTTERFLY

INSPIRING
SEXY
IMAGINATIVE

If you were born on this day:
There is something special about you. People in your presence are inspired to be more than they think they can be. It is part of your make-up to continually grow and evolve, or you begin to feel disconnected from your adventurous spirit.

How this color benefits you:
Your personal color resonates with the gentle and peaceful side of your nature. Wearing, meditating on, or surrounding yourself with Butterfly helps you enjoy every moment in each stage of life that you are experiencing.

Compatible birthdays:
February 9 • May 18 • October 18

Butterfly = PANTONE 12-0322

AMBERGLOW

MAGNIFICENT
DIFFERENT
DARING

If you were born on this day:
Your mind is quick and alert. Everything about you tends to move faster than the rest of the world. You are highly dynamic and not afraid to go where no one has gone before. You can be entertaining and generous, especially with your energy.

How this color benefits you:
Your personal color helps calm your nervous system. It brings you back to your center. Wearing, meditating on, or surrounding yourself with Amberglow helps move you through boredom and restlessness into the deeper and more profound aspects of yourself.

Compatible birthdays:
January 21 • May 22 • May 16

Amberglow = PANTONE 16-1350

OPALINE GREEN

MONEYMAKER
POWERFUL
INFLUENTIAL

If you were born on this day:
People look to you for ideas and inspiration. You are a powerful force and can be an inspirational role model. You are meant to be an expert in whatever profession or goal you choose to pursue. You have the ability to build your dreams and integrate your imagination into a concrete reality.

How this color benefits you:
Your personal color helps you move through times of change and the cycles of life. Wearing, meditating on, or surrounding yourself with Opaline Green helps you know when to take action, when to back up, and when to stay put.

Compatible birthdays:
January 8 • May 2 • September 20

Opaline Green = PANTONE 14-0226

NILE BLUE

OUTGOING
NURTURING
FRIENDLY

If you were born on this day:
You have a restless spirit that craves adventure and challenge. You enjoy recognition and need to feel that you are at the center of things. Love and affection are important to you. It is essential for you to remain open to new opportunities and experiences. Part of your growth comes from dealing with change and unexpected occurrences.

How this color benefits you:
Your personal color resonates with trust and knowledge. Wearing, meditating on, or surrounding yourself with Nile Blue helps ease self-doubt and supports you through times of transition.

Compatible birthdays:
April 18 • April 26 • August 4

Nile Blue = PANTONE 15-5210

MELON

CREATIVE
AFFECTIONATE
SENSUAL

If you were born on this day:
You are a sensual person with a huge appetite for life. You like to live on a grand scale. Whether it is the way you decorate your home, the clothes you wear, or the food you eat, you enjoy luxury and excellence. You like to be in a position of power and want to be adored and appreciated.

How this color benefits you:
Your personal color helps balance any propensity toward excess. Wearing, meditating on, or surrounding yourself with Melon strengthens your center and tempers emotional extremes.

Compatible birthdays:
January 24 • April 9 • December 31

Melon = PANTONE 16-1442

WEDGEWOOD

CREATIVE
YOUTHFUL
EFFICIENT

If you were born on this day:
You have enormous creativity and an eye for detail. Highly principled, you are a good person who takes your work and behavior seriously. You love to learn and acquire information. You are constantly analyzing and assimilating the psychological aspects of life. You can be hard on yourself and need to be surrounded by people who remind you of your greatness and caring nature.

How this color benefits you:
Your personal color resonates with peace and love. Wearing, meditating on, or surrounding yourself with Wedgewood calms your nerves and lightens your spirit.

Compatible birthdays:
March 14 • April 19 • December 22

Wedgewood = PANTONE 18-3935

SPICED CORAL

POWERFUL
BRILLIANT
FOCUSED

JULY 26

If you were born on this day:
You are dynamic and will not take a back seat to anyone. You are extremely intelligent and can absorb and analyze information quickly. Many people born on this day have the ability to make huge amounts of money and can climb steadily to the top of their career. Although you like to do things your way, you have a charm and wit that people find endearing.

How this color benefits you:
Your personal color integrates focus with flow. Wearing, meditating on, or surrounding yourself with Spiced Coral enhances compassion and decreases rigidity.

Compatible birthdays:
January 26 • March 24 • December 15

Spiced Coral = PANTONE 17-1644

FIESTA

ADORABLE
LOVING
FORCEFUL

If you were born on this day:
You have a strong and loving nature, and learning is very important to you. You are not afraid to work long and hard to become an expert in your field of choice. You have an innate love of life, and people find you endearing. Individuals born on this day have a great combination of creativity, compassion, and organizational ability.

How this color benefits you:
Your personal color connects you with your true feelings. Wearing, meditating on, or surrounding yourself with Fiesta brings out the leader and humanitarian within you.

Compatible birthdays:
June 21 • September 25 • December 13

Fiesta = PANTONE 17-1564

CORAL ROSE

DIPLOMATIC
RESOURCEFUL
DEVOTED

If you were born on this day:
You know how to move in and out of social situations with grace and ease. Although you may appear open, you have a private side that you do not share easily with others. You are extremely devoted to those you love and to the social causes that you believe in.

How this color benefits you:
Your personal color helps you move through the challenges that life offers. Wearing, meditating on, or surrounding yourself with Coral Rose increases strength and courage in the face of adversity.

Compatible birthdays:
February 25 • June 17 • December 17

Coral Rose = PANTONE 16-1349

LITTLE BOY BLUE

ROYAL
DILIGENT
EARNEST

If you were born on this day:
People born on this day tend to
be experts in whatever career or
endeavor they choose. You are
mate-oriented and function best
when you are in a healthy relationship. You have an intense nature,
so take care not to become
overly dogmatic.

How this color benefits you:
Your personal color helps dilute
drama and prejudicial ideas or
concepts. Wearing, meditating on,
or surrounding yourself with Little
Boy Blue infuses new energy into
old habits and limiting thought
forms.

Compatible birthdays:
February 27 • April 2 • July 18

Little Boy Blue = PANTONE 16-4132

NECTARINE

FUNNY
UNUSUAL
PHYSICAL

If you were born on this day:
You have a lot of energy and vitality. Most people with this birthday have a physical presence that is attractive and sensual. You have a good sense of humor and are fun to be around. Your optimistic nature helps you move beyond temporary setbacks.

How this color benefits you:
Your personal color resonates with your innocence and self-confidence. Wearing, meditating on, or surrounding yourself with Nectarine helps you move toward your goals with optimism and assurance.

Compatible birthdays:
March 26 • July 8 • December 31

Nectarine = PANTONE 16-1360

BEECHNUT

GENEROUS
WORLDLY
EXCEPTIONAL

If you were born on this day:
People born on this day are fun and interesting to have around. You have an understanding of human nature that allows you to move through social situations without prejudice or restraint. You are not afraid to tell it like it is. Generous and intelligent, you are a great ally and friend.

How this color benefits you:
Your personal color lightens the serious side of your personality. Wearing, meditating on, or surrounding yourself with Beechnut supports monetary growth and good health.

Compatible birthdays:
July 30 • November 11 • November 25

Beechnut = PANTONE 14-0425

SUN ORANGE

REGAL
INSPIRING
POWERFUL

The color for the month of August
is Sun Orange. Grand and royal,
this is a color that resonates with
power and greatness. Gold signifies
both spiritual and material wealth.
During the month of August the sun
moves through the majestic sign
of Leo, the sign that rules royalty.
The brightness of this color dispels
darkness and is especially helpful
when you feel the need to protect
yourself. It also assists in aligning
you with riches, monetary support,
and your position in life.

Sun Orange = PANTONE 16-1257

AUGUST

AUGUST

SUN ORANGE can be used by anyone to increase creativity and joy.

Sun Orange eliminates self-consciousness and allows you to express yourself with radiance and confidence. It opens the heart and lets love enter. This is a color that resonates with laughter and celebration—it is easy to smile when you wear or surround yourself with Sun Orange. This color will lift your mood and allow you to see the brighter side of life.

AUTUMN SUNSET

DEVOTED
PERSISTENT
INTENSE

If you were born on this day:
You function best when you are in a leadership position. You are not one to follow someone else's drumbeat. Loyal and committed, you make your influence felt when you believe in a person or a cause. Because of your royal nature, you need to be treated with respect.

How this color benefits you:
Your personal color supports ease. Wearing, meditating on, or surrounding yourself with Autumn Sunset helps channel your creativity and intensity in a loving and flowing manner.

Compatible birthdays:
May 29 • July 29 • August 13

Autumn Sunset = PANTONE 16-1343

CADMIUM YELLOW

SEXY
COMPLEX
CREATIVE

If you were born on this day:
You are known for your sex appeal, and people love your personality. Creative outlets are necessary to express your passion and purpose to the world. Because of your sensitivity, your moods fluctuate and at times can drain your enthusiasm and energy.

How this color benefits you:
Your personal color helps ground your aspirations. Wearing, meditating on, or surrounding yourself with Cadmium Yellow increases your faith in both yourself and others.

Compatible birthdays:
August 26 • September 20 • December 1

Cadmium Yellow = PANTONE 15-1054

FIRECRACKER

INTERESTING
INTELLIGENT
SEDUCTIVE

AUGUST 03

If you were born on this day:
You have a tremendous amount of charm and wit, and people gravitate to you. Theatrical ability and performing in front of others may come quite naturally to you. You have what it takes to commercialize your talents. Many of you are known for that quiet smile that you usually have on your face.

How this color benefits you:
Your personal color resonates with your warm and loving manner. Wearing, meditating on, or surrounding yourself with Firecracker connects you to your greatness while opening your heart.

Compatible birthdays:
February 13 • March 25 • April 9

Firecracker = PANTONE 16-1452

SUNFLOWER

PRODUCTIVE
DILIGENT
COURAGEOUS

If you were born on this day:
You are not afraid to fight for what you want. You have ability and strength and know how to persevere in the face of adversity. You are a generous and loving person and quietly lend a helping hand to a great many people.

How this color benefits you:
Your personal color helps ease your tenacious spirit. Wearing, meditating on, or surrounding yourself with Sunflower inspires calm as you continue to learn, explore, and attain the many goals you have on your horizon.

Compatible birthdays:
May 21 • September 21 • November 12

Sunflower = PANTONE 16-1054

FELDSPAR

INDEPENDENT
TRUSTWORTHY
KIND

If you were born on this day:
You have many gifts and talents. Your ability to make something out of nothing is awe-inspiring. People like you, and when you feel centered, you can move in and out of professional and social spheres with grace and ease. You need a certain amount of independence and recognition to do a good job.

How this color benefits you:
Your personal color inspires trust and flow. Wearing, meditating on, or surrounding yourself with Feldspar integrates your need for independence with your desire for a loving partnership.

Compatible birthdays:
June 8 • August 31 • December 31

Feldspar = PANTONE 16-5815

CAMELLIA

FUNNY
UNUSUAL
LOVING

If you were born on this day:
You are one of a kind, and there
is no particular mold you fit into.
You are smart yet silly, loving yet
restless, and an interesting combination of contradictions. Highly individual, you need a balance of love,
security, and adventure.

How this color benefits you:
Your personal color resonates with
joy. Wearing, meditating on, or surrounding yourself with Camellia
gives you the inner confidence you
need to move up and out into the
world of possibilities.

Compatible birthdays:
January 22 • September 18 •
October 11

Camellia = PANTONE 16-1541

ASH ROSE

SPIRITUAL
MAGNANIMOUS
EXCEPTIONAL

AUGUST 07

If you were born on this day:
High-minded and generous, you are an angel of society. You care about the world and the people in it. The drive to contribute something to humanity and to follow your soul's purpose is an important part of your makeup. Many people born on this day have the ability to create financial wealth and prosperity.

How this color benefits you:
Your personal color supports good judgment and compassion. Wearing, meditating on, or surrounding yourself with Ash Rose helps balance the physical, emotional, and spiritual aspects of your life.

Compatible birthdays:
January 30 • March 6 • July 24

Ash Rose = PANTONE 17-1514

AZALEA

DYNAMIC
DRAMATIC
CLEVER

If you were born on this day:
You have a convincing and dramatic nature. You are extremely powerful, and when you put your mind to something, you will do nothing short of achieving your goal. You are serious yet playful, and it is this combination that helps you move unscathed through many of life's challenges.

How this color benefits you:
Your personal color calms your intensity. Wearing, meditating on, or surrounding yourself with Azalea combines your passion with spirituality.

Compatible birthdays:
June 8 • September 7 • November 24

Azalea = PANTONE 17-1842

GOLDEN POPPY

DIGNIFIED
DEVOTED
CAPTIVATING

If you were born on this day:
You were born with a special something. A starlike quality radiates from within you. You are a good and loving person. When you care for someone, you care with all your heart. You are empathetic and understand the plight of others.

How this color benefits you:
Your personal color helps you guard against going to excess. Wearing, meditating on, or surrounding yourself with Golden Poppy inspires strength and a renewed sense of hope and self-confidence.

Compatible birthdays:
February 9 • June 17 • October 17

Golden Poppy = PANTONE 16-1462

ARTISAN'S GOLD

EXPRESSIVE
IMAGINATIVE
MUSICAL

If you were born on this day:
Creative expression is vital to your well-being. You are enterprising and know how to envision your goals. You have a mind that is very active and at times can be a little hard to handle. A spiritual connection is important to help you channel the power that you have within.

How this color benefits you:
Your personal color helps you move past worry and self-doubt. Wearing, meditating on, or surrounding yourself with Artisan's Gold inspires a sense of peace and gratitude.

Compatible birthdays:
May 27 • August 27 • October 18

Artisan's Gold = PANTONE 15-1049

GOLD EARTH

PERCEPTIVE
SELF-MOTIVATED
ENLIGHTENING

If you were born on this day:
You have a knack for shining a
light that inspires others. You
illuminate the way through your
own accomplishments or through
the insights and ideas that you
share with those around you.
Striking balances between action
and receptivity and between
independence and partnerships
is a common theme for
people born on this day.

How this color benefits you:
Your personal color blends the
gentle side with the aggressive side
of your nature. Wearing, meditating
on, or surrounding yourself with
Gold Earth enhances intuition and
highlights your mission in life.

Compatible birthdays:
March 10 • April 20 • October 13

Gold Earth = PANTONE 15-1234

FLAMINGO

PRODUCER
ASSERTIVE
ACTIVE

If you were born on this day:
You are a natural go-getter. When you know what you want, you will work long and hard to achieve that goal. You are inspired from within and have a strong spiritual makeup that allows you to move up in the world with faith and assurance. Your life can get hectic, and you may find that you are doing too many things at once.

How this color benefits you:
Your personal color helps balance your home and professional life. Wearing, meditating on, or surrounding yourself with Flamingo replenishes your energy and keeps you from taxing your resources.

Compatible birthdays:
February 13 • March 22 • November 30

Flamingo = PANTONE 16-1450

APRICOT ORANGE

PROVOCATIVE
INNOVATIVE
INDIVIDUALISTIC

If you were born on this day:
You are a student of life and are constantly exploring, evaluating, and probing ideas and ideologies. You have a strong spirit and are not afraid to delve deeply into the heart of matters. You have the ability to overcome life's hurdles and challenges as long as you do not isolate yourself or become too serious.

How this color benefits you:
Your personal color supports your resilience. Wearing, meditating on, or surrounding yourself with Apricot Orange keeps your mind and heart open and available to the love and understanding that can come from others.

Compatible birthdays:
June 8 • July 28 • October 11

Apricot Orange = PANTONE 17-1353

AUGUST 13

TEAL BLUE

POPULAR
FUNNY
PERSISTENT

If you were born on this day:
You have an easygoing manner that belies your strong will. You are your own person and like to do things your own way. Funny and entertaining, you have a wide range of talents. You are a practical and critical thinker. Whether you persevere quietly or are more vocal in your desires, you are rarely thwarted by obstacles or detours.

How this color benefits you:
Wearing, meditating on, or surrounding yourself with Teal Blue honors your individuality yet enhances your interaction with others.

Compatible birthdays:
May 31 • August 17 • September 22

Teal Blue = PANTONE 17-5024

STONEWASH

DRIVEN
TASTEFUL
SENSUAL

AUGUST 15

If you were born on this day:
You are magnetic, and others find you highly attractive. You have impeccable taste, and people look to you to set the trend. You have a sensual nature and may have a talent for cooking or knowing the best restaurants in town. Love is very important to your well-being. Your sensitive nature can work best in a creative field, such as the performing or decorative arts.

How this color benefits you:
Your personal color dissolves fear and excessive sensitivity. Wearing, meditating on, or surrounding yourself with Stonewash enables you to express your talents in a confident and powerful manner.

Compatible birthdays:
April 2 • June 8 • September 25

Stonewash = PANTONE 17-3917

WILD ROSE

POWERFUL
FOCUSED
CREATIVE

If you were born on this day:
You were born to be special, and you have an enormous amount of energy and drive. Your innovative and restless spirit moves you past limitations into the world of magic and miracles. You are a visionary who is not afraid to take risks and who accepts the price of change when the need arises.

How this color benefits you:
Your personal color invokes and amplifies the spiritual side of life. Wearing, meditating on, or surrounding yourself with Wild Rose keeps you connected to the truth and your highest mission in life.

Compatible birthdays:
April 15 • July 29 • September 15

Wild Rose = PANTONE 16-1715

MECCA ORANGE

DEEP
HEALER
PERCEPTIVE

If you were born on this day:
You have an enormous amount of depth and awareness. Capable of seeing what is hidden, you are a light for others as they move through troubled or uncharted waters. Taking action and making mistakes are both important parts of your evolution. Learning to express yourself fearlessly is a life-giving exercise.

How this color benefits you:
Your personal color guards against discouragement and obsession. Wearing, meditating on, or surrounding yourself with Mecca Orange supports joy and renewal.

Compatible birthdays:
March 14 • March 25 • June 17

Mecca Orange = PANTONE 18-1450

RUST

CHARISMATIC
PERSEVERING
SUCCESSFUL

If you were born on this day:
Many people born on this day aspire to great heights and often achieve an enormous amount of wealth and prosperity. Although you value your privacy, being in the limelight may come naturally to you. Creativity is vital to your well-being. Discipline and trust need to be constantly aligned to ensure self-confidence.

How this color benefits you:
Your personal color encourages strength and foresight. Wearing, meditating on, or surrounding yourself with Rust eliminates suspicion and promotes trust so that you can see with clarity.

Compatible birthdays:
February 17 • September 17 • November 26

Rust = PANTONE 18-1248

VIBRANT ORANGE

RHYTHMIC
TENDER
REGAL

If you were born on this day:
Your loving nature makes you a favorite among your peers. Although you can appear very social, you take only a select few into your inner circle. Many people born on this day have a talent for music and dance. You are a great teacher, partner, and friend. Highly romantic, you need someone with whom to share your life and experiences.

How this color benefits you:
Your personal color accentuates your lively spirit. Wearing, meditating on, or surrounding yourself with Vibrant Orange stimulates your style and individuality.

Compatible birthdays:
March 1 • September 26 • October 24

Vibrant Orange = PANTONE 16-1364

MISTLETOE

THOUGHTFUL
MESSENGER
MENTALLY ACTIVE

If you were born on this day:
You have an active mind and a gift for intuition. Highly sensitive, you need to guard against excessive worry and self-doubt. You have a strong sense of duty and function best when you are doing something that makes a difference in the world. Finding a balance between your need to share and your need to remain autonomous is a common theme for those born on this day.

How this color benefits you:
Your personal color emphasizes balance. Wearing, meditating on, or surrounding yourself with Mistletoe soothes mental agitation and worry.

Compatible birthdays:
January 2 • April 2 • May 28

Mistletoe = PANTONE 16-0220

SPICY ORANGE

EXCEPTIONAL
WRITER
SUCCESSFUL

If you were born on this day:
Most people born on this day have a gift for communication. Whether it is through writing or speaking, your verbal acumen is highly regarded. You can jest and play with the best of them. You have a theatrical side and enjoy the spotlight. Productivity and financial security are important to you.

How this color benefits you:
Your personal color brightens your spirit. Wearing, meditating on, or surrounding yourself with Spicy Orange allows you to release pent-up energy and embrace life anew with optimism and receptivity.

Compatible birthdays:
January 20 • June 14 • July 27

Spicy Orange = PANTONE 18-1445

ARABESQUE

INGENIOUS
PLAYFUL
SERIOUS

If you were born on this day:
You are the playful builder. Although you have a logical bent and a serious side to your nature, you must integrate this earnestness with your imagination and lighthearted optimism. It is vital to your well-being to produce tangible results. Taking one step at a time toward your desired dreams is essential.

How this color benefits you:
Your personal color embodies hopefulness and enthusiasm. Wearing, meditating on, or surrounding yourself with Arabesque helps you stay open to new ideas and alternatives.

Compatible birthdays:
February 21 • June 3 • December 12

Arabesque = PANTONE 16-1441

SEA GREEN

MAGICAL
DRAMATIC
SPIRITED

If you were born on this day:
You are a dreamer, and it is important that your life be filled with ideas and moments of greatness. The dull and mundane will not hold your interest for long. It is important that you take the necessary time to develop the skills to augment the innate talents that you already possess. To be great, you need to be courageous enough to make mistakes.

How this color benefits you:
Your personal color resonates with adventure and introspection. Wearing, meditating on, or surrounding yourself with Sea Green helps you feel grounded and self-assured.

Compatible birthdays:
March 17 • October 21 • December 17

Sea Green = PANTONE 16-5421

GRAPE NECTAR

COMPLEX
BRIGHT
RESPONSIBLE

If you were born on this day:
You enjoy learning and want to be stimulated mentally. You have creative ability and will feel most satisfied when you are expressing your unique talents. Your senses are acute, and you are very aware of your surroundings. Having things of beauty around you gives you great pleasure.

How this color benefits you:
Your personal color embodies strength, passion, and persever-ance. Wearing, meditating on, or surrounding yourself with Grape Nectar helps you move through fear so that you can enjoy the fruits of your labor.

Compatible birthdays:
May 3 • June 5 • November 14

Grape Nectar = PANTONE 18-1710

VERY GRAPE

SMART
PERFORMER
GENTLE

If you were born on this day:
No matter how tough you may appear, you are a gentle soul. You have healing abilities and may be drawn to a career that helps others. You have a great imagination and are also suited for the performing arts. Try not to focus on what you perceive to be your inadequacies.

How this color benefits you:
Your personal color embodies sweetness. Wearing, meditating on, or surrounding yourself with Very Grape inspires courage and connects you to the beauty of life.

Compatible birthdays:
January 18 • June 7 • December 15

Very Grape = PANTONE 18-3220

CORAL GOLD

LOYAL
TENACIOUS
HUMANITARIAN

If you were born on this day:
You are a kind and loving person. You are always willing to lend a helping hand. You feel best when you are connected to people who believe in you. You have a strong sense of responsibility and will work long and hard to try to do a good job. You need to know that you are appreciated.

How this color benefits you:
Your personal color radiates strength. Wearing, meditating on, or surrounding yourself with Coral Gold helps you acknowledge and appreciate your own worth.

Compatible birthdays:
July 14 • September 21 • December 28

Coral Gold = PANTONE 16-1337

MUSKMELON

LOVING
IDEALISTIC
TOLERANT

If you were born on this day:
People born on this day are not afraid to give. Generosity is something that comes quite naturally to you. What you cannot give from your pocket you will give from your heart. You can be overly responsible at times and can wear yourself out. Travel and learning are two areas that can help replenish your spirit.

How this color benefits you:
Your personal color resonates with the qualities of optimism and responsibility. Wearing, meditating on, or surrounding yourself with Muskmelon increases your energy and connects you to your inner radiance.

Compatible birthdays:
January 8 • May 8 • September 26

Muskmelon = PANTONE 15-1242

AUGUST 28

APRICOT

STYLISH
BIGHEARTED
INDEPENDENT

If you were born on this day:
You have a strong sense of individuality and do not follow others easily.
You have a talent for looking good,
and people will look to you to set
trends. You are stylish and innovative,
and you dress and act the way you
want. You are bighearted, and love
plays an important role in your life.

How this color benefits you:
Your personal color embodies the
qualities of both excitement and
serenity. Wearing, meditating on,
or surrounding yourself with
Apricot connects you to the
nectar of life.

Compatible birthdays:
February 18 • April 27 •
November 9

Apricot = PANTONE 15-1153

GREEN OASIS

DETAIL-ORIENTED
PROFOUND
KIND

If you were born on this day:
You have style and flair and carry yourself with confidence. You always look good. Your outer assurance is very different from your sensitive core. Deep and perceptive, you have a rare combination of insight and honesty that is not always embraced and that is often misunderstood.

How this color benefits you:
Your personal color resonates with bravery. Wearing, meditating on, or surrounding yourself with Green Oasis helps you move through disappointments and imperfections with trust and ease. It is a reminder that the continual progression of life is where perfection reigns.

Compatible birthdays:
January 10 • January 21 • July 30

Green Oasis = PANTONE 15-0538

JAFFA ORANGE

ANALYTICAL
RESPONSIBLE
SENSITIVE

If you were born on this day:
You love to use your mind. Your ability to analyze problems and situations is exceptional. You never really know just how good or talented you are due to your yearning for perfection. Many people born on this day cover their sensitivity with facts and a composed exterior. You have a very sensitive spirit that needs to be nurtured and recognized.

How this color benefits you:
Wearing, meditating on, or surrounding yourself with Jaffa Orange helps you live life more freely by integrating your intellect with your emotions and your passion with self-control.

Compatible birthdays:
March 19 • August 24 • November 26

Jaffa Orange = PANTONE 16-1454

PEACH BLOOM

DETERMINED
DYNAMIC
ASTUTE

If you were born on this day:
You are a builder of dreams. Whether it is through a career, family, or home, you want to manifest your heart's desire. You are driven and want to be in control. Your thirst for knowledge is something that will keep you young and active.

How this color benefits you:
Your personal color supports your tender and loving nature. Wearing, meditating on, or surrounding yourself with Peach Bloom calms your nervous system, especially when you are feeling overwhelmed.

Compatible birthdays:
January 12 • May 8 • May 21

Peach Bloom = PANTONE 15-1327

SEPTEMBER

BAJA BLUE

DIVINE
DISCERNING
ARTISTIC

The color for the month of September is Baja Blue. This is a divine and alluring color that resonates with beauty, purity, and wisdom. Mercury and then Venus move through the heavens during the month of September. This is a time when our thinking and our appreciation of beauty is heightened. Baja Blue increases our breadth of scope. It can help ease tension and promote tranquility. This color opens the mind to higher concepts and a less limiting point of view.

Baja Blue = PANTONE 18-3946

BAJA BLUE can be used by anyone to help discern information.

Baja Blue blends intelligence with peace and wisdom while refining your communication skills. This color can purify your thinking and help integrate the big picture with the little picture. Use it when you need help organizing your life. Surround yourself with Baja Blue to increase your aesthetic abilities and awaken your sense of beauty.

SEPTEMBER

SMOKE BLUE

EFFICIENT
ORGANIZED
SMART

If you were born on this day:
Your gentle and friendly personality belies your keen intellect and inner strength. You are hardworking and loyal. The people you befriend or work with are lucky to have you in their lives. Although you have an independent nature, you take your relationships very seriously. You are generous with your energy and support.

How this color benefits you:
Your personal color balances the emotional and intellectual parts of you. Wearing, meditating on, or surrounding yourself with Smoke Blue helps you integrate work with play and flexibility with responsibility.

Compatible birthdays:
March 27 • May 19 • July 27

Smoke Blue = PANTONE 17-4412

DAYBREAK

SUPPORTIVE
INSPIRED
GENEROUS

SEPTEMBER 02

If you were born on this day:
You are a person who is bright and caring. You have a giving nature and are a supportive friend. You reach great heights when you are stimulated and inspired. It is important for you to pursue your dreams with practical tenacity, or you may feel restless and unsatisfied.

How this color benefits you:
Your personal color vibrates with ideals and protection. Wearing, meditating on, or surrounding yourself with Daybreak helps you move through fear and indecision with ease and agility.

Compatible birthdays:
February 20 • March 29 • November 20

Daybreak = PANTONE 17-3817

SEPTEMBER 03

GRAPEADE

RESOURCEFUL
TALENTED
PLAYFUL

If you were born on this day:
You know how to get what you want, and you pursue your ambitions relentlessly. Although you may appear playful and easygoing, you take your interests seriously. You are resourceful and will work long and hard to accomplish your aims. People find you attractive and charismatic.

How this color benefits you:
Your personal color helps calm your nervous system. Wearing, meditating on, or surrounding yourself with Grapeade connects you to others in a healthy and harmonious manner.

Compatible birthdays:
January 30 • April 9 • December 12

Grapeade = PANTONE 18-3211

AQUA

HARDWORKING
WRITER
ANALYTICAL

If you were born on this day:
You are extremely perceptive and able to grasp complex subjects. You love to learn and explore new ideas. Try not to separate yourself from others in your attempt to stay centered and in control. Creating a proper balance between giving too much of yourself and becoming isolated can be a challenge. You have a strong spiritual calling, and when connected to your mission in life, you can be a great healer.

How this color benefits you:
Your personal color invokes peace and ease. Wearing, meditating on, or surrounding yourself with Aqua inspires trust and breadth of vision.

Compatible birthdays:
June 22 • October 21 • November 16

Aqua = PANTONE 15-4717

NEPTUNE GREEN

IMAGINATIVE
YOUTHFUL
THEATRICAL

If you were born on this day:
You have a sensual and charismatic personality. It is important that you don't allow monetary concerns to become the focal point in your life, or you may waste precious time doing things that are not supportive of your true calling.

How this color benefits you:
Your personal color helps bridge the romantic with the responsible side of your nature as you form new relationships and endeavors. Wearing, meditating on, or surrounding yourself with Neptune Green helps you break unhealthy patterns and gives you the courage to take action.

Compatible birthdays:
January 5 • February 5 • June 12

Neptune Green = PANTONE 14-6017

VERONICA

KIND
ARTISTIC
SEARCHER

If you were born on this day:
People born on this day are kind and compassionate. You have a giving and generous spirit. Artistically inclined, you want and need to express your talents. You long for a truthful and authentic life and are continually learning and striving to become a better friend, mate, and person.

How this color benefits you:
Your personal color helps you move through past hurts and anger. Wearing, meditating on, or surrounding yourself with Veronica helps balance your life with discipline, self-love, and compassion.

Compatible birthdays:
January 24 • March 19 • August 6

Veronica = PANTONE 18-3834

SEPTEMBER 06

DAHLIA PURPLE

GOOD-LOOKING
DISCRIMINATING
VERBAL

If you were born on this day:
You are smart and discriminating and tend to choose your words carefully. You have an understanding of true beauty and good health. Although you are outgoing and friendly, it is not always easy for people to get to know you on a deep level. You save the more intimate parts of yourself for a chosen few.

How this color benefits you:
Your personal color helps calm your restless nature. Wearing, meditating on, or surrounding yourself with Dahlia Purple helps quiet the mind while connecting you to happiness.

Compatible birthdays:
January 8 • April 27 • October 27

Dahlia Purple = PANTONE 17-3834

ETRUSCAN RED

RESOURCEFUL
CHARMING
INTELLIGENT

SEPTEMBER 08

If you were born on this day:
You are aware of what you want
and are not shy about getting it.
Your charm and intelligence help you
move in and out of social circles
with style and flair. Your mind is
sharp, and you crave mental stimulation. You love to learn and find
education extremely valuable. It is
important to remember that the
perfection of life is limitless and
cannot always be controlled.

How this color benefits you:
Your personal color corresponds
with depth, vitality, and passion.
Wearing, meditating on, or surrounding yourself with Etruscan Red
inspires you to move through life
with energy and wisdom.

Compatible birthdays:
March 8 • September 19 •
October 18

Etruscan Red = PANTONE 18-1434

SEPTEMBER 09

GRAPE ROYALE

INTENSE
PROVOCATIVE
MYSTIC

If you were born on this day:
You have a complex nature and are not satisfied with the superficial. Something inside of you longs for more meaning. Discipline, action, and flexibility should be integrated for you to feel calm and balanced. Deep emotions should be explored with love and compassion or your thoughts can become negative or antagonistic.

How this color benefits you:
Your personal color helps you release limiting thoughts and beliefs. Wearing, meditating on, or surrounding yourself with Grape Royale connects you to your royal nature. It helps activate your intuition and your strong sense of truth.

Compatible birthdays:
March 9 • September 21 • November 7

Grape Royale = PANTONE 19-3518

JADESHEEN

UNUSUAL
CREATIVE
LEADER

If you were born on this day:
You have a nice combination of practicality and idealism. Your mind is quick, and you can handle most situations with dexterity and leadership ability. You have a nature that vibrates with class and royalty. It is important for you to have a spiritual connection to life or you may feel lonely or separate.

How this color benefits you:
Your personal color resonates with enthusiasm and encouragement. Wearing, meditating on, or surrounding yourself with Jadesheen helps ease monetary concerns and integrates love with financial security.

Compatible birthdays:
February 21 • August 9 • December 16

Jadesheen = PANTONE 16-6324

SEPTEMBER 11

INFINITY

HARDWORKING
COMPLEX
BEAUTIFUL

If you were born on this day:
People born on this day are naturally kind and good-natured. You are charismatic and artistic. You are not afraid to work hard and often must be reminded to take a break. Partnerships are very significant to you, and it is therefore important for you to form happy and healthy relationships.

How this color benefits you:
Your personal color aligns you with peace and perfection. Wearing, meditating on, or surrounding yourself with Infinity helps you move through doubt and indecision while increasing self-confidence and your sense of trust.

Compatible birthdays:
January 29 • June 6 • October 11

Infinity = PANTONE 17-4015

MEADOW

PRINCIPLED
HARDWORKING
ASTUTE

SEPTEMBER 12

If you were born on this day:
Your quiet intelligence combined with an ability to size up a situation allow you to achieve many of your goals. It is important to cultivate a spiritual alliance and to take frequent breaks in your daily tasks. Your mind tends to work overtime, so exercise and meditation are very helpful in keeping you balanced and optimistic. Although you have a practical side, there is an inspired part of you that holds some of your greatest potential.

How this color benefits you:
Your personal color resonates with trust and success. Wearing, meditating on, or surrounding yourself with Meadow helps you move through life with peace and joy.

Compatible birthdays:
May 8 • June 6 • September 21

Meadow = PANTONE 14-6319

BERYL GREEN

DETERMINED
KNOWLEDGEABLE
QUICK-WITTED

If you were born on this day:
You have a strong and determined nature. A mundane life is not for you. It is important for you to connect with others and exchange information. You have a way with words, and whether writing or speaking, you are able to captivate an audience by telling a good story.

How this color benefits you:
Your personal color represents good fortune. Wearing, meditating on, or surrounding yourself with Beryl Green aids in receptivity and opens your heart to love and companionship.

Compatible birthdays:
January 7 • April 22 • August 27

Beryl Green = PANTONE 16-5515

HORIZON BLUE

GENEROUS
DEVOTED
SENSITIVE

SEPTEMBER 14

If you were born on this day:
You have a kind heart and a strong feeling nature that should be expressed in a creative manner. It is important for you to infuse joy and amusement into your everyday activities. You are not afraid to fight for a cause. Although you tend to excel in many areas, it is sometimes difficult for you to appreciate your own worth.

How this color benefits you:
Your personal color helps lighten your spirit. Wearing, meditating on, or surrounding yourself with Horizon Blue dissolves feelings of loneliness and increases flexibility and joy.

Compatible birthdays:
August 18 • September 27 • November 12

Horizon Blue = PANTONE 16-4427

TULIPWOOD

GREGARIOUS
SENSUAL
WARM

If you were born on this day:
You have a warm and friendly personality. You are giving in social situations and often take up the slack or fill in the gaps in conversations. Due to your sensual nature, you may have a propensity toward excess. Food, drink, and other sensual activities can take up a lot of your time and energy.

How this color benefits you:
Your personal color helps you resonate with true beauty and pleasure. Wearing, meditating on, or surrounding yourself with Tulipwood reduces procrastination and dissolves worry.

Compatible birthdays:
January 19 • March 6 • December 15

Tulipwood = PANTONE 18-1709

ELDERBERRY

REFINED
POETIC
TEACHER

If you were born on this day:
You have a refined and highly aesthetic nature. Your love of learning keeps you alert and makes you a great source of information for your friends and loved ones. You have a natural understanding of healing, art, beauty, and design.

How this color benefits you:
Your personal color increases self-confidence and supports the spiritual side of your nature. Wearing, meditating on, or surrounding yourself with Elderberry tempers envy and dramatic behavior patterns while infusing your thoughts with love and understanding.

Compatible birthdays:
March 31 • July 16 • August 30

Elderberry = PANTONE 17-1605

TABASCO

ANALYTICAL
POWERFUL
DISCRIMINATING

If you were born on this day:
Your serious and persistent nature ensures a substantial amount of success. You are not afraid to work hard, and you go after your goals with a relentless drive. Many people born on this day carry a great deal of responsibility. A fun and loving spirit should be cultivated and embraced.

How this color benefits you:
Your personal color combines passion with duty. Wearing, meditating on, or surrounding yourself with Tabasco helps you see and hear with your heart, where truth and happiness reside.

Compatible birthdays:
June 17 • July 8 • September 26

Tabasco = PANTONE 18-1536

AUTUMN LEAF

INTENSE
SUCCESSFUL
QUESTIONING

SEPTEMBER 18

If you were born on this day:
Your mind is quick and alert. You are constantly learning while challenging ideas, concepts, and people. You are a hard worker and a good executive. Your eye for detail can be a gift or a challenge, depending on how you use it.

How this color benefits you:
Your personal color highlights perception and trust. Wearing, meditating on, or surrounding yourself with Autumn Leaf eases worry, enhances self-discipline, and aligns you with the cycles of life.

Compatible birthdays:
February 18 • August 31 • December 18

Autumn Leaf = PANTONE 17-1347

SEPTEMBER 19

CACTUS

RESEARCHER
HEALER
SEDUCTIVE

If you were born on this day:
You are an interesting and provocative person with strong principles
and a seductive nature. The truth is
very important to you. You are
constantly challenging yourself and
others to work toward an idea of
perfection. You are a natural
researcher and can do well in any
area once you put your mind to it.

How this color benefits you:
Your personal color enhances
mental ease while protecting your
boundaries. Wearing, meditating on,
or surrounding yourself with Cactus
increases your gratitude and recognition for all the teachers and life
experiences you have encountered.

Compatible birthdays:
February 19 • April 9 • July 3

Cactus = PANTONE 18-0130

SILT GREEN

CAPABLE
POPULAR
INSPIRING

If you were born on this day:
People like to be in your company.
You are inspiring and often prolific.
You want to be fair while using a
healthy balance of perception and
intelligence. It is important
for you to have a partner
who is kind and loving.

How this color benefits you:
Your personal color resonates with
peace and calm. Wearing, meditating on, or surrounding yourself
with Silt Green replenishes your
energy and balances your mind,
body, and spirit.

Compatible birthdays:
February 12 • June 14 •
December 26

Silt Green = PANTONE 14-5706

GRAPE SHAKE

WHEELER-DEALER
WRITER
PRODUCER

If you were born on this day:
You have many talents that can be used in a variety of endeavors. You have a great sense of humor and like to channel your creative intelligence in myriad ways. There is so much that you can do once you set your sights on a goal. You are innovative and ambitious, and it is important for you to develop self-assurance.

How this color benefits you:
Your personal color calms uncertainty. It merges passion with detachment. Wearing, meditating on, or surrounding yourself with Grape Shake honors and balances your complex nature.

Compatible birthdays:
February 9 • May 27 • December 18

Grape Shake = PANTONE 18-2109

MISTY ROSE

UNUSUAL
DYNAMIC
CLEVER

If you were born on this day:
Your mind is sharp and clever. You appear strong and self-confident, and you do not show your vulnerability easily. It is important for you to have someone with whom you can relate. Sharing and exploring life's questions are important parts of your journey.

How this color benefits you:
Your personal color eases irritation and connects you to love and passion. Wearing, meditating on, or surrounding yourself with Misty Rose heightens your receptivity and aligns your interests with meaning and purpose.

Compatible birthdays:
August 13 • November 24 • December 22

Misty Rose = PANTONE 15-1512

SKY BLUE

FAIR
ARTISTIC
COMPASSIONATE

If you were born on this day:
You are an instrument of light and love. You are highly principled, with a refined nature, and anything that is crude or base is antagonistic to your system. You have a strong sense of fair play and find it difficult to associate with people who are unscrupulous. Whether you are viewing works of art or creating them yourself, you have a good eye for detail.

How this color benefits you:
Your personal color embodies the qualities of peace and calm. Wearing, meditating on, or surrounding yourself with Sky Blue helps you pierce through hurt and anger and align with vision and possibility.

Compatible birthdays:
March 23 • May 14 • July 28

Sky Blue = PANTONE 14-4318

CORNFLOWER BLUE

ROMANTIC
EMOTIONAL
MUSICAL

If you were born on this day:
Love is very important to you, as is
the need to connect with others.
You are highly romantic and function
best when you are in a healthy
relationship. Although you can be
emotional, you have a keen mind
and a sharp wit. Harmony and
a happy home and family hold
great comfort for you.

How this color benefits you:
Your personal color resonates with
clarity. Wearing, meditating on, or
surrounding yourself with
Cornflower Blue lends discrimination
to your ability when choosing
partners and close associates.

Compatible birthdays:
January 28 • June 15 • June 24

Cornflower Blue = PANTONE 16-4031

SEA FOG

RESEARCHER
SOCIALLY CONSCIOUS
ARTICULATE

If you were born on this day:
You are good at whatever you do. Your natural inclination to do things well puts you in a position to excel. People are attracted to you and listen to your point of view. You have an analytical mind and are capable of investigating and understanding truths, trends, and people.

How this color benefits you:
Your personal color vibrates at a high level. Wearing, meditating on, or surrounding yourself with Sea Fog keeps you connected to others and aware of your vital place in the world.

Compatible birthdays:
January 25 • August 16 • October 14

Sea Fog = PANTONE 16-3304

PLUM WINE

INTENSE
CHARISMATIC
IMAGINATIVE

If you were born on this day:
A life filled with love is very important to you. People feel better when you are around. Try not to let disappointments dull your natural enthusiasm. Transformation is an integral part of your life. Although some experiences can be challenging, you can count on them to move you toward your soul's purpose.

How this color benefits you:
Your personal color helps increase strength and perception. Wearing, meditating on, or surrounding yourself with Plum Wine sustains your spirit by increasing resolve.

Compatible birthdays:
January 26 • September 24 • December 16

Plum Wine = PANTONE 18-1411

SEPTEMBER 26

RENAISSANCE ROSE

PROGRESSIVE
EFFICIENT
INDEPENDENT

If you were born on this day:
The need to be great and to do something significant is inherent in the people born on this day. Independence is highly prized, and doing things your own way is important to you. People tend to adore you and are willing to follow your lead.

How this color benefits you:
Your personal color holds the qualities of greatness and humility and connects you to your higher self. Wearing, meditating on, or surrounding yourself with Renaissance Rose calms doubts and insecurities so that you can lead with love and compassion.

Compatible birthdays:
January 28 • July 18 • October 27

Renaissance Rose = PANTONE 18-1613

BOK CHOY

ATTRACTIVE
DEPENDABLE
HARDWORKING

If you were born on this day:
You are highly magnetic, and people find you attractive. You are a wonderful friend, mate, or ally, once someone has earned your loyalty. You are not afraid to work, and you often delight in a job well done.

How this color benefits you:
Your personal color helps you release old thoughts and out-moded behavior patterns. Wearing, meditating on, or surrounding yourself with Bok Choy helps you resonate with your perfection and reminds you of the magic that you have within.

Compatible birthdays:
January 19 • October 19 • December 10

Bok Choy = PANTONE 13-6208

SEPTEMBER 28

DREAM BLUE

INTELLIGENT
RESOURCEFUL
COLORFUL

If you were born on this day:
You have a creative mind and an adventurous spirit. It may be a challenge for you to keep your equilibrium due to your sensitive nature. Partnerships are very important to you, and you should surround yourself with people who are kind and loving. It is essential for you to be creative and express your childlike spirit. Don't allow the responsibilities of life to weigh you down.

How this color benefits you:
Your personal color resonates with vision. Wearing, meditating on, or surrounding yourself with Dream Blue eases your emotional nature and promotes balance and well-being.

Compatible birthdays:
January 21 • July 18 • August 11

Dream Blue = PANTONE 15-4005

DUSK

WITTY
POWERFUL
TALENTED

SEPTEMBER 30

If you were born on this day:
You have tremendous magnetism, and people gravitate to you with ease. Your powerful personality helps you move through social circles with agility. Interacting with others is a valuable part of your life. You gain recognition easily, so it is important that you channel your artistic and dramatic talents toward a desired goal.

How this color benefits you:
Your personal color supports reflection and cooperation. Wearing, meditating on, or surrounding yourself with the color Dusk tempers intensity and points you in the right direction toward relationships and goals.

Compatible birthdays:
May 12 • August 20 • August 31

Dusk = PANTONE 17-3812

OCTOBER

CERULEAN

PEACEFUL
POISED
BALANCED

The color for the month of October is Cerulean. Calm and soothing, Cerulean signifies love, beauty, and balance. Cerulean embodies the essence of peace and serenity while inspiring us to be strong and take decisive action. Venus, the planet that rules the month of October, governs love and beauty. This is a great month to enhance your physical appearance or beautify your surroundings.

Cerulean = PANTONE 15-4020

CERULEAN can be used by anyone to achieve peace and calm.

Cerulean is the color that helps attract harmonious relationships. It promotes ease while allowing you to attain a proper balance between giving and receiving. Use it when seeking harmony in your environment. By calming aggressive tendencies, the color can be useful when mediating on an irritating situation. Use Cerulean to add splendor and beauty to your surroundings.

OCTOBER

PURPLE HEATHER

LEADER
ORGANIZER
DECISION MAKER

If you were born on this day:
Leadership roles await you, as the numeral 1 in your birthday denotes self-reliance and precision. There is a great deal that you can accomplish with your strong and independent nature. You carry the qualities of strength and vitality and have the necessary power to get the job done.

How this color benefits you:
Your personal color enhances your charisma and allure. Wearing, meditating on, or surrounding yourself with Purple Heather blends your strength of purpose with kindness, and your independence with cooperation.

Compatible birthdays:
January 5 • March 1 • April 2

Purple Heather = PANTONE 14-3911

KENTUCKY BLUE

FAIR
DISCERNING
MEDIATOR

If you were born on this day:
Your ability to see both sides of a situation makes you a favorite when it comes to telling it like it is. You are the one to be trusted and to judge fairly. Your ability to retain information and use it when needed is uncanny. You are intelligent and mate-oriented. Strive to keep things new and exciting, and avoid getting stuck in a routine that is too limiting for your true nature.

How this color benefits you:
Your personal color reminds you to stay flexible. Wearing, meditating on, or surrounding yourself with Kentucky Blue balances your emotional needs with the analytical side of your nature.

Compatible birthdays:
January 30 • February 19 • November 20

Kentucky Blue = PANTONE 15-3915

ORCHID BOUQUET

COMMUNICATIVE
SOCIAL
EXPRESSIVE

If you were born on this day:
You lead with style and flair and have the ability to get the party going. Fashion, dance, and the arts are just some of the many fields you can pursue. It is important to stay grounded and have a secure base from which to function. Remember that love and relationships need care and attention. No matter how far your spirit soars, it is always better to share your experiences with others.

How this color benefits you:
Your personal color helps align you with your mission in life. Wearing, meditating on, or surrounding yourself with Orchid Bouquet supports your need for freedom as well as your need for security and stability.

Compatible birthdays:
June 25 • November 3 • December 1

Orchid Bouquet = PANTONE 15-3412

HEATHER

REALISTIC
SERIOUS
FUNNY

If you were born on this day:
There is a logical and serious side to your nature, combined with a wild sense of adventure and childlike wonder. It is important for you to honor both sides as you move through life. Work is your greatest ally, as you build your dreams and create a bridge between the spirit and the material worlds. Dance, law, comedy, and the healing arts are just some of the careers that you may enjoy.

How this color benefits you:
Your personal color helps you balance the spiritual with the mundane. Wearing, meditating on, or surrounding yourself with Heather supports a sense of magic as you pursue your personal and professional goals.

Compatible birthdays:
June 9 • September 23 • December 14

Heather = PANTONE 14-4110

WINSOME ORCHID

SPARKLY
INTELLIGENT
OUTGOING

If you were born on this day:
You are creative and articulate and want to share your ideas and observations with others. Popularity can come quickly as you step forth and express your sensitivity and intelligence. You fight for the rights of others and are quick to oppose unfairness. Be true to your own unique personality as you step out into the world and connect with people.

How this color benefits you:
Your personal color stimulates bravery. Wearing, meditating on, or surrounding yourself with Winsome Orchid activates your courage and charisma as you spread the word of freedom, compassion and understanding.

Compatible birthdays:
April 15 • July 24 • September 19

Winsome Orchid = PANTONE 14-3206

GRAPEMIST

SENSUAL
ROMANTIC
ARTISTIC

If you were born on this day:
You are creative and magnetic and have a flair for performing or doing anything that requires imagination. A healthy lifestyle and creative outlets that allow you to express yourself are vital. Your daily schedule is important. The sensual part of your personality can push you toward excess if you are not mindful.

How this color benefits you:
Your personal color vibrates to the many facets of your personality. Wearing, meditating on, or surrounding yourself with Grapemist enables you to feel balanced in the midst of the numerous changes that occur from day to day.

Compatible birthdays:
September 7 • September 28 • November 16

Grapemist = PANTONE 16-3929

OCTOBER 07

LANGUID LAVENDER

CHARISMATIC
ARTICULATE
SOCIALLY CONSCIOUS

If you were born on this day:
A strong belief system and eloquent intelligence make you an attractive and charismatic person. You are often devoted to a cause, so it is important for you to have some quiet time alone to regroup and recuperate. Taking a walk or swim can move you through any agitation or irritable feelings. Being by the water can be especially soothing. Although there can be a struggle between independence and part-nership, both should be honored.

How this color benefits you:
Wearing, meditating on, or sur-rounding yourself with Languid Lavender helps you maintain your individuality as you embrace the rewards of balanced relationships.

Compatible birthdays:
January 13 • March 17 • August 17

Languid Lavender = PANTONE 15-3910

MULBERRY

SEXY
DEEP
PROBING

If you were born on this day:
Your ability to delve below the surface is your specialty. You are a natural investigator and can see things through to the core of the truth. You have a natural talent for attracting money. Romantic and sensual, you are irresistible to many people. You were born with strength and capability.

How this color benefits you:
Wearing, meditating on, or surrounding yourself with Mulberry helps you sustain your passion without becoming too intense.

Compatible birthdays:
March 9 • June 7 • November 18

Mulberry = PANTONE 17-3014

OCTOBER 08

SMOKY GRAPE

PASSIONATE
LEADER
ROMANTIC

If you were born on this day:
You are creative and dynamic and are meant to do great things. You have a lot of magnetism and can be an inspiration to others. It is important for you to learn how to handle the large amount of energy that runs through your system. Similar to a racecar driver, you need to harness and steer that dynamic power.

How this color benefits you:
Your personal color helps you direct your life in a way that enables you to give back to society. Wearing, meditating on, or surrounding yourself with Smoky Grape helps balance your wisdom and passion with purpose and direction.

Compatible birthdays:
March 1 • May 4 • November 1

Smoky Grape = PANTONE 16-3110

DUSTY PINK

ANALYTICAL
INTELLIGENT
PERFORMER

If you were born on this day:
You are innovative and direct in your approach to life. You can succeed in most endeavors and are gifted in many ways. The need for independence combined with your need to share your experiences with a significant partner can be challenging at times. The solution includes balancing your head with your heart.

How this color benefits you:
Your personal color helps you move through any emotional indecision. Wearing, meditating on, or surrounding yourself with Dusty Pink helps you transform your innovative ideas into great works of art.

Compatible birthdays:
February 2 • March 10 • March 22

Dusty Pink = PANTONE 14-1316

OCTOBER 11

VIOLA

INTUITIVE
FAIR
IMAGINATIVE

If you were born on this day:
You are intuitive and sensitive.
You have a propensity for design
and choreography, and creating a
more beautiful world is one of your
innate talents. It is important for you
to share your life with others. Love
and partnerships contribute to your
feeling happy and balanced. Try to
make beauty and peace a part of
your surroundings.

How this color benefits you:
Your personal color accentuates
your natural grace and elegance.
Wearing, meditating on, or surrounding yourself with Viola helps
you move through any fear or
indecision you may have.

Compatible birthdays:
April 3 • June 12 • September 12

Viola = PANTONE 16-3815

EGGSHELL BLUE

POPULAR
CLEVER
EXPRESSIVE

If you were born on this day:
You are socially adept, and people love to have you at their gatherings. You absorb data easily, and your mind is quick as a whip. You need to be stimulated and exposed to different types of people and experiences. The challenge is to know how and when to communicate and to be conscious of what you are saying to others.

How this color benefits you:
Your personal color helps balance your active intelligence with intuitive wisdom. Wearing, meditating on, or surrounding yourself with Eggshell Blue reminds you to mix your interactions with love and good cheer.

Compatible birthdays:
March 12 • September 13 • November 12

Eggshell Blue = PANTONE 14-4809

OCTOBER 13

OPAL BLUE

PRACTICAL
BUILDER
DRIVEN

If you were born on this day:
You are capable of handling huge amounts of responsibility. You can work tirelessly as long as you can see the fruits of your labor. Although you can do things very well on your own, it is often better to align your objectives with those of others. Home and family are important to your well-being. Try to stay light-hearted, and do not allow your goals to dictate all your waking hours.

How this color benefits you:
Wearing, meditating on, or surrounding yourself with Opal Blue lightens the serious side of your nature while helping to realize your dreams.

Compatible birthdays:
June 5 • September 14 • November 23

Opal Blue = PANTONE 12-5406

STARLIGHT BLUE

PERSUASIVE
DIGNIFIED
ENTERTAINER

OCTOBER 14

If you were born on this day:
You have a keen eye for beauty, decoration, and style. It is good for you to communicate your ideas to the public. You can be eloquent when speaking to an audience. People are attracted to your visions and will support you in many ways. Take time out for relaxation, and try not to scatter yourself in too many directions.

How this color benefits you:
Wearing, meditating on, or surrounding yourself with Starlight Blue helps unite your mental acumen with spiritual awareness.

Compatible birthdays:
February 6 • April 24 • September 15

Starlight Blue = PANTONE 12-4609

LILAC SNOW

SENSITIVE
ARTISTIC
SENSUAL

If you were born on this day:
You have a gift for storytelling and an appreciation for beauty. The performing arts can be a great vehicle for your many talents. You can do well in front of an audience, especially if the words you speak resonate within your heart. You have a strong magnetism that makes you attractive to others. It is important to surround yourself with people and objects that promote harmony.

How this color benefits you:
Your personal color enhances your imagination. Wearing, meditating on, or surrounding yourself with Lilac Snow helps you set limits and boundaries while reminding you not to get caught up in too many of life's dramas.

Compatible birthdays:
April 25 • July 7 • September 16

Lilac Snow = PANTONE 13-3405

LAVENDER

AESTHETIC
PERSEVERING
ENCHANTED

If you were born on this day:
Your ability to connect people with one another is astounding. You succeed in opening the eyes and ears of those around you, whether you are adding style to a friend's wardrobe or sharing the hidden truth about a political atrocity. You have excellent taste and a discerning eye. Be aware of any addictive tendencies, for they can appear unusually seductive.

How this color benefits you:
Your personal color helps you stay balanced. Wearing, meditating on, or surrounding yourself with Lavender helps guard you against unwanted influences and reminds you to save some time for yourself.

Compatible birthdays:
February 8 • March 26 • June 17

Lavender = PANTONE 15-3817

ORCHID SMOKE

TRANSFORMING
POWERFUL
SEDUCTIVE

If you were born on this day:
Your ability to transform yourself and others is extremely powerful. You like to push past limits and go where no man or woman has gone before. There is a great deal of restlessness in your birth date. Try to incorporate ease into your daily plans, because too much intensity can be hard on your body. You can use your curiosity to discover valuable information.

How this color benefits you:
Wearing, meditating on, or surrounding yourself with Orchid Smoke allows you to explore profound experiences while sustaining a balanced and secure foundation.

Compatible birthdays:
April 9 • June 27 • December 27

Orchid Smoke = PANTONE 15-2210

LIGHT LILAC

BREAKTHROUGHS
COLORFUL
PROFOUND

If you were born on this day:
Being the best is often a calling for those born on this day. You have an unusual depth of purpose that must be channeled. You have a natural disinterest in anything average. You are colorful and expressive; wall-flowers need not apply. Structure is needed to help you reach your destination. Remind yourself to appreciate life's softer notes and experiences.

How this color benefits you:
Wearing, meditating on, or sur-rounding yourself with Light Lilac gives you strength to endure as you encounter the more mundane parts of the journey, which are present no matter how high the goal or reward.

Compatible birthdays:
February 1 • September 9 • December 10

Light Lilac = PANTONE 12-2903

BURNT CORAL

INNOVATIVE
INDEPENDENT
COMMUNICATOR

If you were born on this day:
You have an independent nature coupled with a need for companionship. You may experience a few interesting relationships before you feel that you have truly met your match. The need for balance in all areas of life is the challenge. You are a true thinker, and it is important that you don't get too attached to your own point of view.

How this color benefits you:
Wearing, meditating on, or surrounding yourself with Burnt Coral helps you stay flexible and optimistic as you unravel and explore the riddles and truths of a fulfilling life.

Compatible birthdays:
February 11 • August 20 • November 2

Burnt Coral = PANTONE 16-1529

COSMIC SKY

ARTISTIC
INTUITIVE
RESILIENT

If you were born on this day:
You have an uncanny ability to predict trends in fashion, music, and art. You have a refined nature and therefore dislike anything that is too crude or coarse. There is often a conscious or subconscious longing for your other half, a special mate or life partner. You want people in your life with whom you can share your heart, soul, and ideas.

How this color benefits you:
Wearing, meditating on, or surrounding yourself with Cosmic Sky promotes faith in finding your significant other and decreases the inclination to worry.

Compatible birthdays:
March 3 • April 21 • July 12

Cosmic Sky = PANTONE 15-3909

CHINTZ ROSE

VERBAL
INSPIRING
MUSICAL

If you were born on this day:
Your mental powers are highly developed. Many individuals with this birthday are meant to share information with people from all walks of life and from all over the world. People who are rich or poor, from the city or the country, all seem to be able to hear you. Sometimes you think too much, especially when you don't get enough physical exercise or have any creative outlets.

How this color benefits you:
Your personal color can help channel your thoughts into constructive endeavors. Wearing, meditating on, or surrounding yourself with Chintz Rose balances the emotional with the intellectual side of your nature.

Compatible birthdays:
August 22 • October 4 • December 31

Chintz Rose = PANTONE 13-1408

DUSTY AQUA

BUILDER
CHARISMATIC
DESIRABLE

If you were born on this day:
You are a natural ruler and builder and can create things of beauty. People may look to you as a role model, for you can appear regal and in control. It is important to blend leadership with cooperation to acknowledge and honor this position.

How this color benefits you:
Your personal color reminds you that love should take precedence over duty. Wearing, meditating on, or surrounding yourself with Dusty Aqua helps you ground your aspirations with regard to love and family.

Compatible birthdays:
February 5 • March 11 • June 14

Dusty Aqua = PANTONE 12-5506

HEIRLOOM LILAC

ELOQUENT
FUNNY
AGILE

If you were born on this day:
Far deeper than you may appear, you have what it takes to go the distance. There is a lot more to you than meets the eye. You have a nice blend of wit and sensitivity and are known for your timing. You are meant to communicate and entertain and are unusually magnetic in front of an audience. Take care of the people dearest to you without giving away all your energy.

How this color benefits you:
Wearing, meditating on, or surrounding yourself with Heirloom Lilac reminds you to save time for yourself to relax and rejuvenate.

Compatible birthdays:
April 24 • June 24 • October 15

Heirloom Lilac = PANTONE 16-3812

REGAL ORCHID

MAGNETIC
INSPIRING
YOUTHFUL

If you were born on this day:
Your optimism and strength of purpose are an inspiration to others. You are a catalyst for change and transformation. You are known for telling it like it is, and those closest to you can always count on you to tell them the truth. People want you in their corner, and you are fiercely loyal to those you love or believe in.

How this color benefits you:
Your personal color reminds you of your greatness. Wearing, meditating on, or surrounding yourself with Regal Orchid helps you retain your optimism and poise as you interact with others who are not always as versatile or resourceful as you are.

Compatible birthdays:
March 16 • June 9 • August 16

Regal Orchid = PANTONE 16-3525

RED VIOLET

REFLECTIVE
SPIRITUAL
INDIVIDUALISTIC

If you were born on this day:
Many people born on this day have a quiet strength that lies just below the surface. Your ability to focus and commit to a dream can make you a winner. Athletics is an area in which you may excel. Although you need to love and relate to others, you require a certain amount of time when you can be alone to find your own unique path.

How this color benefits you:
Your personal color can help you embody strength and sensitivity. Wearing, meditating on, or surrounding yourself with Red Violet encourages balance and poise.

Compatible birthdays:
August 8 • December 8 • December 23

Red Violet = PANTONE 17-1818

BARBERRY

POWERFUL
SEXY
INTENSE

OCTOBER 26

If you were born on this day:
Fluent and articulate, you can be a great speaker and advocate for rights. You are not afraid to step up to the plate. Adversity will not claim you or stop you from creating and attaining your desires and aspirations. Resist the urge to allow power to intoxicate you. Use your strength as a tool to get the job done and to spread your words effectively.

How this color benefits you:
Wearing, meditating on, or surrounding yourself with Barberry helps integrate your intensity and commitment with clarity and ease.

Compatible birthdays:
February 27 • May 9 • July 20

Barberry = PANTONE 18-1760

MOLTEN LAVA

DYNAMIC
COURAGEOUS
PROFOUND

If you were born on this day:
You are deep and probing, and your mind needs a way of channeling itself. A tremendous amount of energy runs through your system. Connecting your perceptions to a cause can help focus and direct your ambitions. Learning how to do things step by step is an important factor in regulating your power and speed.

How this color benefits you:
Your personal color helps you navigate through the emotional aspects of life. Wearing, meditating on, or surrounding yourself with Molten Lava reminds you to stay calm and centered.

Compatible birthdays:
March 7 • May 5 • August 11

Molten Lava = PANTONE 18-1555

BAROQUE ROSE

COMMITTED
INNOVATIVE
COMPLEX

OCTOBER 28

If you were born on this day:
A born leader, you are not afraid to work hard or initiate action. You are focused and direct. You are highly individualistic, and it is sometimes difficult for you to follow the rules of others. Partnerships need to be honored and understood.

How this color benefits you:
Wearing, meditating on, or surrounding yourself with Baroque Rose allows you to trust and blend with people who are close to you while encouraging you to retain your individuality.

Compatible birthdays:
March 2 • May 22 • September 11

Baroque Rose = PANTONE 18-1634

BEAUJOLAIS

DEVOTED
PERCEPTIVE
PERSUASIVE

If you were born on this day:
You are often perceptive and funny and usually get what you want because of your interesting person- ality. The ability to disarm people with your wit and intelligence is remarkable. Try not to cover fear or insecurity with arrogance or a sharp tongue.

How this color benefits you:
Wearing, meditating on, or sur- rounding yourself with Beaujolais reminds you to combine ease with strategy and intention.

Compatible birthdays:
July 21 • September 30 • December 4

Beaujolais = PANTONE 18-2027

CARDINAL

COMMUNICATIVE
REFLECTIVE
ADVENTURER

If you were born on this day:
Playful and generous, you have a
natural desire to share your gifts
with others. You are a born explorer.
The need to roam and to learn new
things is pronounced in your date of
birth. A life that has enough variety
in it is important to you. People tend
to gravitate toward your personality.

How this color benefits you:
Wearing, meditating on, or
surrounding yourself with Cardinal
helps you sustain the qualities
of flow and stability as
you enjoy life's adventures.

Compatible birthdays:
March 29 • May 28 • August 31

Cardinal = PANTONE 18-1643

OCTOBER 30

TIBETAN RED

AUSPICIOUS
MAGICAL
PRACTICAL

If you were born on this day:
Your courage and persistence will help you attain many of life's blessings. Once you are interested in something, you have the necessary willpower and tenacity to attain it. Seeing the fruits of your labor is vital to your well-being. You are a born detective and appreciate a challenge.

How this color benefits you:
Wearing, meditating on, or surrounding yourself with Tibetan Red helps you sink your teeth into something while remaining lighthearted and flexible during the journey.

Compatible birthdays:
January 4 • August 23 • October 22

Tibetan Red = PANTONE 19-1934

CLARET RED

INTENSE
PASSIONATE
TRANSFORMING

The color for the month of November is Claret Red. Intense and passionate, this color inspires depth, strength, and love. People born during this month can see beyond the mundane and into the hearts of others. This is a great color to use when integrating perception with a more lighthearted detachment. Claret Red helps you stay inspired as you build your dreams and ambitions.

Claret Red = PANTONE 17-1740

NOVEMBER

CLARET RED can be used by anyone to help move through a transformation.

Claret Red embodies the qualities of love and passion. It can add a sexual lift to your life. Use it to remove emotional blocks that are in your way or when you face a difficult passage. This color also promotes physical love and helps awaken the libido. Surround yourself with Claret Red to increase passion, conviction, and emotional fortitude.

MARS RED

COMMANDING
DYNAMIC
ENTERPRISING

NOVEMBER 01

If you were born on this day:
You were born to explore and investigate, and it is important for you to be exposed to new and interesting ideas. You want to be offered opportunities for growth and understanding. Your mind is keen and alert. Try to stay curious and open to alternative points of view. You can be a great leader if you cultivate the ability to be flexible.

How this color benefits you:
Your personal color allows you to move into new territory with an open mind. Wearing, meditating on, or surrounding yourself with Mars Red helps you integrate persistence with adaptability.

Compatible birthdays:
March 6 • June 23 • September 18

Mars Red = PANTONE 18-1655

NOVEMBER 02

RASPBERRY WINE

EMPATHETIC
TRANSFORMING
RESPONSIBLE

If you were born on this day:
People born on this day tend to
carry a great deal of responsibility.
You care deeply for those closest
to you and often are of service to
those in need. People come to you
for advice and understanding.

How this color benefits you:
Your personal color helps you
move through the emotional
turbulence that can occur as life
unfolds. Wearing, meditating on, or
surrounding yourself with Raspberry
Wine reminds you to stay on
course and not allow others to sap
all your energy.

Compatible birthdays:
September 4 • October 21 •
November 11

Raspberry Wine = PANTONE 18-1741

CHINESE RED

PERCEPTIVE
KIND
MAGNETIC

If you were born on this day:
People find you attractive and magnetic. There is much that you can see and understand with regard to human nature. Although you have an uncanny ability to know people, you keep most of your observations to yourself. Adventurous and secretive, you need to be on the move. Resist the urge to hold on to hurt feelings.

How this color benefits you:
Your personal color connects you to your strength and kindles your urge for the new and untried. Wearing, meditating on, or surrounding yourself with Chinese Red encourages initiative, flexibility, and persistence.

Compatible birthdays:
April 29 • May 3 • July 17

Chinese Red = PANTONE 18-1663

NOVEMBER 03

AMERICAN BEAUTY

SOLID
GIVING
CREATIVE

If you were born on this day:
Enormously creative, you are able to excel in many areas. You are well liked by those who know you and are a wonderful addition to any endeavor with which you connect. Loyal and loving, you need to guard against doing too much. Your ability to give from your heart is what is most notable about you. You convey the feeling of home and family to those who need it most.

How this color benefits you:
Your personal color combines passion with duty. Wearing, meditating on, or surrounding yourself with American Beauty reminds you to give from a centered space, to rest more often, and to receive when the time is right.

Compatible birthdays:
January 23 • March 30 • October 5

American Beauty = PANTONE 19-1759

JESTER RED

ENTERTAINING
QUICK
INTELLIGENT

If you were born on this day:
Your gift with words and nuances can be quite dazzling. You need to be connected with nature and the outdoors. Although your mind is active and alert, being close to nature moves you toward wisdom and away from the trappings of overthinking. Miracles happen when you connect with trust and quiet.

How this color benefits you:
Your personal color helps you pierce through confusion and restlessness. Wearing, meditating on, or surrounding yourself with Jester Red inspires patience and knowing.

Compatible birthdays:
February 14 • March 4 • December 13

Jester Red = PANTONE 19-1862

NOVEMBER 05

DEEP CLARET

DEEP
SENSUAL
DEVOTED

If you were born on this day:
Your ability to understand the thoughts and feelings of others is one of your strong points. You are able to convey many things through your words and creative talents. Many people born on this day have a great deal of courage and persistence. People find you attractive and likable. Fighting for a cause often brings out the best in your character.

How this color benefits you:
Your personal color reminds you of your true nature. Wearing, meditating on, or surrounding yourself with Deep Claret helps you combine a sense of purpose with a charismatic ease.

Compatible birthdays:
May 30 • October 7 • December 17

Deep Claret = PANTONE 19-1840

CHILI PEPPER

SPIRITUAL
HEALER
KNOWLEDGEABLE

If you were born on this day:
You can help many people if you keep true to the spiritual part of your nature. It is important for you to stay connected to generous and loving people, as partnerships are an intricate part of your life and happiness. Writing, the study of medicine, and sharing yourthoughts with others are all activities that resonate with your innate gifts.

How this color benefits you:
Your personal color helps balance your intellect with your emotions. Wearing, meditating on, or surrounding yourself with Chili Pepper reminds you to stay centered as you connect with others and to share your point of view with an open heart.

Compatible birthdays:
February 25 • October 8 • December 6

Chili Pepper = PANTONE 19-1557

RED BUD

POWERFUL
CHARISMATIC
REGAL

If you were born on this day:
Strong and capable, you often help others by leading the way. As you make your mark in the world, remember to be open to the new and untried. Be persistent but not stubborn and your leadership will be embraced and admired by others. You are an investigator at heart and are able to discern truth from fiction if you choose to do so.

How this color benefits you:
Your personal color helps you let go of the old and welcome the new. Wearing, meditating on, or surrounding yourself with Red Bud severs psychological bonds that can be constricting to your nature.

Compatible birthdays:
January 2 • August 2 • October 1

Red Bud = PANTONE 19-1850

PERSIAN RED

DRAMATIC
PROVOCATIVE
COLORFUL

NOVEMBER 09

If you were born on this day:
Your dramatic personality can bring you into the public eye. You can be very influential to others, so it is important that you channel your energy in a well-meaning and balanced manner. Too much intensity can cloud the truth, and it is the truth for which you really long. You have a lighthearted side that needs to be honored. A good sense of humor can bring many benefits.

How this color benefits you:
Your personal color aligns with the receptive side of your nature. Wearing, meditating on, or surrounding yourself with Persian Red helps you to attract good fortune.

Compatible birthdays:
March 13 • April 25 • August 26

Persian Red = PANTONE 19-1860

AURORA RED

LEADER
COMMUNICATOR
APPEALING

If you were born on this day:
Inspired communication is one of the many talents you have. Writing, speaking, and teaching are just some of the ways you can help illuminate others. You can be very determined, so it is best that you have somewhere to channel your desires. Guard against a stubborn streak.

How this color benefits you:
Wearing, meditating on, or surrounding yourself with Aurora Red reminds you to stay flexible and grounded as you build your dreams into a manifested reality.

Compatible birthdays:
January 2 • February 19 • October 13

Aurora Red = PANTONE 18-1550

MALAGA

INTUITIVE
PROFOUND
IMAGINATIVE

NOVEMBER 11

If you were born on this day:
Your combination of strength
and sensitivity is most intriguing.
Working with others is an important
part of your evolution. Although you
are self-confident and a force to be
reckoned with, it is your close relationships that give you the insights
necessary to live in a more fruitful
and balanced manner. Creative
expression is one of the keys to
your well-being and can bring
great rewards.

How this color benefits you:
Wearing, meditating on, or
surrounding yourself with Malaga
helps you move through any
intense interactions with
confidence and trust.

Compatible birthdays:
April 13 • June 22 • September 16

Malaga = PANTONE 17-1723

NOVEMBER 12

BAKED APPLE

DETERMINED
ALLURING
INTERESTING

If you were born on this day:
You are mysterious, and a lot of what you feel remains hidden from others. You are mentally strong and have a knack for knowing how to read people. It is very important for you to stay physically active. Sports, dance, and exercise are just some of the ways that you can channel your intensity and release unwanted stress.

How this color benefits you:
Your personal color accentuates your natural charm and sense of humor. Wearing, meditating on, or surrounding yourself with Baked Apple lightens some of your intense feelings and inspires dignity and kindness.

Compatible birthdays:
January 4 • July 14 • August 5

Baked Apple = PANTONE 18-1648

MAGENTA HAZE

STRONG
CARING
INSIGHTFUL

If you were born on this day:
Kind and caring, you are able to share insights and information in the most unusual ways. Your personality tends to promote change and transformation. It is the unique blend of your depth of understanding and the speed and acumen of your intellect that surprises people and makes you a great asset to humanity.

How this color benefits you:
Your personal color reminds you to stay flexible and open to new ideas and information. Wearing, meditating on, or surrounding yourself with Magenta Haze inspires you to share words of truth with your community and the world.

Compatible birthdays:
May 10 • September 6 • October 13

Magenta Haze = PANTONE 18-2525

RED CLAY

UNIQUE
EXPRESSIVE
ARTISTIC

If you were born on this day:
Inspiring to others, you are able to have a great impact on the world around you. It is your unique point of view that helps transcend boundaries and opens the eyes of others. Being by the water supports your need to feel relaxed and calm.

How this color benefits you:
Your personal color helps you observe life with a detached and loving eye. Wearing, meditating on, or surrounding yourself with Red Clay helps erode the illusion of separateness that tends to dominate our physical world and reminds you that we are all connected and operating as one.

Compatible birthdays:
March 16 • September 25 • November 25

Red Clay = PANTONE 18-1454

GARNET ROSE

INSTINCTIVE
SEXY
ADMIRED

If you were born on this day:
Gentle, strong, and challenging are just some of the ways to describe you. Your senses are heightened, and therefore you see many things that the rest of the world does not. It is a gift that, if channeled properly, allows you to find great pleasure. Although you need time alone to replenish your energy, it is important not to hide or isolate.

How this color benefits you:
Your personal color reminds you to honor your gifts by sharing them with others. Wearing, meditating on, or surrounding yourself with Garnet Rose helps you transform any hurts into fertilizer for creation.

Compatible birthdays:
April 22 • May 3 • June 13

Garnet Rose = PANTONE 18-1633

NOVEMBER 15

SLATE ROSE

PENETRATING
UNUSUAL
INDEPENDENT

If you were born on this day:
There is something unusual or exotic in your manner. You are definitely not a run-of-the-mill type of person. Your inner world is deep and mysterious. It may be hard to get to know you, because you keep much of what you feel to yourself. That is not to say that you will not fight for a cause and speak your mind. Knowing who you truly are is reserved for a select and special few.

How this color benefits you:
Your personal color helps stabilize your feelings. Wearing, meditating on, or surrounding yourself with Slate Rose helps you move through life with trust and freedom.

Compatible birthdays:
May 7 • June 1 • October 16

Slate Rose = PANTONE 18-1635

POMPEIAN RED

STRONG
INNOVATIVE
TRANSFORMING

NOVEMBER 17

If you were born on this day:
You are not the type of person to take things lying down. You are a fighter and a formidable foe. You have come into this world to make a difference. People may not always know how you feel, but they know where you stand with regard to your opinions and your ideas. It is important for you to remember that life has cycles. Make friends with change and you will feel freer.

How this color benefits you:
Your personal color combines the qualities of integrity and passion. Wearing, meditating on, or surrounding yourself with Pompeian Red reminds you to lead others with care and support.

Compatible birthdays:
February 20 • May 5 • June 28

Pompeian Red • PANTONE 18-1658

AMARANTH

MAJESTIC
INSIGHTFUL
DETERMINED

If you were born on this day:
Dramatic and perceptive, you are interesting to watch and be around. You strive for greatness, and you have a lot of talent. Partnerships are important to you. Try not to judge yourself or others harshly. Creative development takes time. It is the journey toward your greatness that should be reveled in and enjoyed.

How this color benefits you:
Your personal color heightens your internal power. Wearing, meditating on, or surrounding yourself with Amaranth helps you stay open to intimate relationships without losing yourself.

Compatible birthdays:
January 27 • March 18 • August 9

Amaranth = PANTONE 19-2410

RED OCHRE

INDEPENDENT
ALLURING
FEISTY

NOVEMBER 19

If you were born on this day:
It is very hard for anyone to tell you what to do. You tend to dance to your inner song. Although your independence is a wonderful quality, it is important that you don't shut other people out. Compassion for yourself should be cultivated. Goals and career ambitions will be easy for you to achieve. It is the emotional area of life that needs to be honored and maintained.

How this color benefits you:
Wearing, meditating on, or surrounding yourself with Red Ochre helps you feel safe, centered, and secure.

Compatible birthdays:
April 29 • May 2 • December 19

Red Ochre = PANTONE 18-1442

ROSE WINE

MUSICAL
EXPRESSIVE
IMAGINATIVE

If you were born on this day:
You have a strong feeling nature that allows you to pick up impressions easily. You are good at many things, so it is important for you to be exposed to a variety of interests. You may find that you are usually doing two things at once. Many people born on this day have a talent for music, dance, or the arts. You have a quiet strength that is just below the surface, which you can access when needed.

How this color benefits you:
Your personal color helps you guard against fear and self-doubt. Wearing, meditating on, or surrounding yourself with Rose Wine supports focus and commitment.

Compatible birthdays:
June 23 • September 22 • October 19

Rose Wine = PANTONE 17-1623

GARNET

FUNNY
INTELLIGENT
PASSIONATE

If you were born on this day:
Many people find you delightful
and irresistible. You are smart and
charming. Your mind is always working, and although you keep many of
your perceptions to yourself, you are
constantly assimilating insights and
information. Having a career that
brings you out into the world is
probably best. You are a strong
communicator, and people tend to
listen to what you have to say.

How this color benefits you:
Wearing, meditating on, or
surrounding yourself with Garnet
helps you move in and out of
the public eye while maintaining
a strong sense of self.

Compatible birthdays:
March 5 • August 26 • December 2

Garnet = PANTONE 19-1655

HEATHER ROSE

CAPTIVATING
PRODUCER
UNUSUAL

If you were born on this day:
People born on this day tend to
do things their own way. You have
a keen intellect and a strong will.
You have strong opinions, and you
dislike people who are petty or
superficial. There is a need to share
your knowledge and to have some
degree of prominence. Because of
your self-reliant persona, not everyone is aware of the sensitivity you
have within.

How this color benefits you:
Wearing, meditating on, or
surrounding yourself with Heather
Rose helps balance the masculine
and feminine sides of your nature.

Compatible birthdays:
February 1 • April 4 • October 12

Heather Rose = PANTONE 17-1608

BORDEAUX

SPIRITUAL
APPEALING
WISE

If you were born on this day:
Many people with this birthday are born as old souls, carrying a certain amount of knowledge that takes others a lifetime to discover or understand. Staying flexible and detached is important to your evolution. Being free to study and learn and to connect with a wide range of people brings out the best in you. Success comes easily through discipline and enthusiasm.

How this color benefits you:
Wearing, meditating on, or surrounding yourself with Bordeaux reminds you to allow love to be the motivating force behind all your relationships and endeavors.

Compatible birthdays:
March 7 • June 13 • August 23

Bordeaux = PANTONE 17-1710

DRY ROSE

PROFOUND
EXOTIC
COMMITTED

If you were born on this day:
You have a giving nature and, at times, may feel that you are not appreciated. Try to remember that you are loved, and not everyone knows how to or has the capacity to go the distance the way you do. You are highly creative and understanding. Many people will come to you for support.

How this color benefits you:
Your personal color protects your energy. Wearing, meditating on, or surrounding yourself with Dry Rose supports your compassionate side while allowing you to handle responsibilities with ease.

Compatible birthdays:
June 2 • October 10 • December 2

Dry Rose = PANTONE 18-1725

MAUVE ORCHID

HERO
IDEALISTIC
PERSUASIVE

If you were born on this day:
You can appear flexible and accommodating, but you never take your eye off the ball. No matter how congenial you seem to be, you know where you are going and how you will get there. You can enjoy many different phases as you move through your life. It is important to bless each step you take toward the new and unexplored.

How this color benefits you:
Your personal color can be used as a compass. Wearing, meditating on, or surrounding yourself with Mauve Orchid supports the spiritual side of your nature and helps you move through transitions with peace and trust.

Compatible birthdays:
March 20 • July 17 • September 27

Mauve Orchid = PANTONE 16-2111

VALERIAN

EXCITING
POWERFUL
UNIQUE

If you were born on this day:
No one sees things exactly the way you do. It is this unique perspective that is part of your greatness and often part of your contribution to the world. Courageous and strong, you are not afraid of the unknown or the untried. Born to lead, you often help others see new perspectives. You have the gift of power and therefore the ability to help transform others.

How this color benefits you:
Your personal color helps you channel that power with wisdom and responsibility. Wearing, meditating on, or surrounding yourself with Valerian helps ease any obsessive tendencies and reminds you to stay lighthearted.

Compatible birthdays:
April 28 • July 1 • October 9

Valerian = PANTONE 17-3410

THISTLE DOWN

EXCITING
PROPHETIC
DYNAMIC

If you were born on this day:
You are someone who can light up a room, and "wow" is one of the best ways to describe you. Your energy is felt easily and can be used to excite and stimulate others. You have a rich inner world that not everyone sees, but it is your public persona to which people most often relate.

How this color benefits you:
Your personal color helps you integrate your inner and outer worlds. Wearing, meditating on, or surrounding yourself with Thistle Down removes the illusion of separateness and guides you toward receiving gifts and benefits from others.

Compatible birthdays:
February 2 • February 10 • September 18

Thistle Down = PANTONE 16-3930

ARAGON

COMMUNICATOR
SHARP
QUICK-WITTED

If you were born on this day:
You are quick and charming, and people tend to find you both interesting and challenging. You have a gift for communication and therefore can do very well as an entertainer, writer, or leader, especially in thought-inspiring occupations. Because of your persuasive manner, there is much you can accomplish.

How this color benefits you:
Wearing, meditating on, or surrounding yourself with Aragon allows your sensitivity to blend with your courage and intelligence.

Compatible birthdays:
February 29 • August 7 • December 6

Aragon = PANTONE 17-1532

LAVENDER VIOLET

IMAGINATIVE
BUILDER
VISIONARY

If you were born on this day:
You are capable of making magic. Your intuitive insights, coupled with your ability to manifest your ambitions, are some of your greatest assets to both yourself and others. Try not to juggle too much or be pulled toward indecision.

How this color benefits you:
Your personal color inspires vision and confidence. Wearing, meditating on, or surrounding yourself with Lavender Violet reminds you to build your dreams one step at a time.

Compatible birthdays:
February 12 • October 16 • November 4

Lavender Violet = PANTONE 17-3924

NOVEMBER 30

SAXONY BLUE

EXPLORER
ACTIVIST
WRITER

If you were born on this day:
People love to be around your
curiosity and intelligence. You can
work a party or a social engagement
like nobody's business. Freedom
and movement are very important
for your well-being. You are a natural
writer and communicator.

How this color benefits you:
Your personal color helps calm your
restless nature. Wearing, meditating
on, or surrounding yourself with
Saxony Blue is both grounding
and uplifting and helps you thrive
in the moment.

Compatible birthdays:
April 13 • May 31 • October 13

Saxony Blue = PANTONE 18-4225

PAGODA BLUE

WISDOM
TRUTH
VISION

The color for the month of December is Pagoda Blue. Deep and meditative, this color signifies wisdom, truth, and optimism. Pagoda Blue lends vision and trust to those who wear it. It is a great color to use while traveling or exploring. The color is a useful aid in dealing with others who have alternative points of view.

Pagoda Blue = PANTONE 17-4724

DECEMBER

DECEMBER

PAGODA BLUE
can be used by
anyone on a
spiritual journey.

Pagoda Blue connects information
to truth and wisdom. It helps us to
understand ideas that are different
from our own and to believe that
the truth will be revealed. Pagoda
Blue can be used for travel and
exploration or when you are longing
for a mystical adventure. Wearing it
can lend trust and confidence to
your visions.

BAYOU

OUTGOING
OPTIMISTIC
GROUNDED

If you were born on this day:
Fiery and spontaneous, you are a blast to be around. You were born to perform, communicate, and explore. It is important for you to travel and make yourself available to new people and unusual ideas. No matter how far you roam, however, it is important for you to have a home to which you can return. Roots and a loving environment give you the necessary foundation to go out into the world.

How this color benefits you:
Wearing, meditating on, or surrounding yourself with Bayou supports your need for adventure while reminding you to maintain a sense of security.

Compatible birthdays:
May 28 • July 24 • October 17

Bayou = PANTONE 18-5121

ADRIATIC BLUE

GRAND
SENSITIVE
DARING

If you were born on this day:
Sensitive yet courageous, you are a force to be reckoned with. People find you entertaining and quick-witted. There may be a tendency for you to juggle and get stuck doing two things at once. Whether you live in two different places or you feel torn between two romantic partners, it is important for you to know how to channel your energy in one direction.

How this color benefits you:
Wearing, meditating on, or surrounding yourself with Adriatic Blue helps you focus and make decisions that are truthful and beneficial for you.

Compatible birthdays:
March 22 • May 28 • August 9

Adriatic Blue = PANTONE 17-4320

CELESTIAL

PRIVATE
INDEPENDENT
QUICK-MINDED

DECEMBER 03

If you were born on this day:
Although you are independent and strong, there is a sensitive side of you that remains hidden. It is that side that needs to be acknowledged and understood, because it holds many of your deepest wishes. Try not to hide your feelings, especially from those who are trying so desperately to understand you. Many people born on this day have a gift for dance and music.

How this color benefits you:
Your personal color helps blend your inner and outer worlds. Wearing, meditating on, or surrounding yourself with Celestial helps increase your ability to receive the love you want and need.

Compatible birthdays:
June 26 • July 12 • October 30

Celestial = PANTONE 18-4530

CANTON

POWERFUL
DYNAMIC
INTROSPECTIVE

If you were born on this day:
Charming and intelligent, you tend to watch people intently. Although you may engage in conversations, you are often reticent when it comes to sharing your private thoughts. You value time spent alone and with the people who mean the most to you. The need to build a secure financial base is important to your well-being. Your ambition should be channeled so that you can accomplish your personal and professional aspirations.

How this color benefits you:
Wearing, meditating on, or surrounding yourself with Canton allows you to flow more easily and dissolve any feelings of separation.

Compatible birthdays:
June 5 • August 10 • October 5

Canton = PANTONE 16-5112

RIVIERA

COURAGEOUS
OUTSPOKEN
INTELLIGENT

DECEMBER 05

If you were born on this day:
You are talented and persuasive, and there is much that you can accomplish once you put your mind to it. You are a natural achiever; you expect to win and often do. You want to move around and connect with interesting and important people. As if in a game or a sporting event, you want to play with people who are on your level or better.

How this color benefits you:
Your personal color blends your depth with wisdom. Wearing, meditating on, or surrounding yourself with Riviera reminds you to stay lighthearted and enjoy the game.

Compatible birthdays:
June 19 • July 17 • November 19

Riviera = PANTONE 17-4027

DECEMBER 06

DUSK BLUE

PERCEPTIVE
SMART
PLAYFUL

If you were born on this day:
You are expressive and dramatic, and no one can tell a story like you can. You have a great imagination and a verbal flair that makes people remember you. Many people born on this day have had a lot of success in the sports world. It is the challenge and the achievement of goals that really excite you.

How this color benefits you:
Wearing, meditating on, or surrounding yourself with Dusk Blue reminds you to stay balanced and to understand that moderation can be a helpful tool, not a boring prescription.

Compatible birthdays:
June 6 • June 17 • July 15

Dusk Blue = PANTONE 16-4120

CENDRE BLUE

UNUSUAL
LEADER
CREATIVE

If you were born on this day:
You have a knack for leading without force. People gravitate to you and find you interesting and inspiring. Although you have a great deal of sensitivity, your desire to try new things helps you move through fear and insecurity. The performing arts are just one of the ways you can channel your creative talents.

How this color benefits you:
Wearing, meditating on, or surrounding yourself with Cendre Blue helps you integrate your strength of purpose with your vivid imagination.

Compatible birthdays:
May 19 • October 10 • November 8

Cendre Blue = PANTONE 17-4131

ORIENT BLUE

INTUITIVE
DEEP
PROFOUND

If you were born on this day:
Your depth of perception is one of
your many gifts. Superficial conver-
sation will not hold your attention.
You long for truth in your encounters
with others. Your honesty is not
always welcomed, but it is almost
always a vehicle for transformation.
You function well when you are communicating your perceptive insights
to a large audience. Writing, speaking, and playing music are some of
the many talents you may possess.

How this color benefits you:
Wearing, meditating on, or surrounding yourself with Orient Blue reminds
you that life is about renewal and that
every ending precedes a beginning.

Compatible birthdays:
April 3 • July 19 • August 18

Orient Blue = PANTONE 19-3947

VELVET MORNING

COMMUNICATOR
INSIGHTFUL
PENETRATING

If you were born on this day:
There is no cookie cutter that molds your shape. You are different, and you like it that way. Born to intrigue others and give them a little shock now and then, you are quite a character. You are a great friend and a fierce ally. You can be sensitive and articulate or blunt and cutting, depending on the situation or purpose. Try to focus your energy out into the world, where you can make a difference.

How this color benefits you:
Your personal color helps you channel your intensity. Wearing, meditating on, or surrounding yourself with Velvet Morning gives you the necessary strength to take action and make a difference in the world.

Compatible birthdays:
March 26 • May 30 • September 27

Velvet Morning = PANTONE 18-3927

PORCELAIN GREEN

INNOVATIVE
WISE
GRACIOUS

If you were born on this day:
You can achieve many things due to your inner conviction. You have a propensity for financial gain and worldly success if you are able to stay centered. Balancing the mental and emotional areas of your life is one of your challenges. Many people born on this day have a quiet intelligence and are always listening and learning.

How this color benefits you:
Your personal color helps you channel your ideas into words of inspiration and creations of beauty. Wearing, meditating on, or surrounding yourself with Porcelain Green helps you to stay balanced.

Compatible birthdays:
April 19 • June 28 • August 16

Porcelain Green = PANTONE 17-5421

DELFT

SPIRITUAL
CREATIVE
INSPIRING

If you were born on this day:
Spiritually aware, you were born to make a difference. You may hear your calling early in life. You may not know exactly what you are going to do, but you know that it is special. It is important not to dissipate your energy through fear or indecision. Usually indecision comes from self-doubt.

How this color benefits you:
Your personal color helps you heed your calling. Wearing, meditating on, or surrounding yourself with Delft reminds you to replenish your natural resources with faith and trust.

Compatible birthdays:
May 28 • June 12 • October 17

Delft = PANTONE 19-4039

LYONS BLUE

IMAGINATIVE
CHARISMATIC
SOCIAL

If you were born on this day:
You are known for your charisma
and ease; people just can't get
enough of you. You have a style
and flair that others love to be near.
Many people born on this day make
great performers. You may have
a tendency to push the envelope, a
result of your innate love of life.

How this color benefits you:
Your personal color embodies the
qualities of spontaneity and perfection. Wearing, meditating on, or
surrounding yourself with Lyons
Blue can help you explore life to
the fullest without going to excess.

Compatible birthdays:
March 6 • August 31 • September 28

Lyons Blue = PANTONE 19-4340

GALAPAGOS GREEN

DRAMATIC
PRECISE
EMOTIONAL

If you were born on this day:
You tend to work very hard at what you believe in. Although you have a great sense of humor, you have a serious and emotional streak that lies just under the surface. Part of this complexity is what makes you so attractive to others, but it can also be difficult for you to handle. The integration of your inner long-ings into your daily life holds the key to your well-being and happiness.

How this color benefits you:
Wearing, meditating on, or surrounding yourself with Galapagos Green enhances your ability to persevere with joy and enthusiasm.

Compatible birthdays:
July 12 • September 30 • October 31

Galapagos Green = PANTONE 18-5725

GREEN-BLUE SLATE

COMPLEX
QUICK-WITTED
EXPRESSIVE

If you were born on this day:
Perceptive and intellectually gifted, you can read people quite easily. You often know just what to say or do to give people what they want. You are expressive and funny, and people enjoy it when you entertain them. It is important for you to discover your own wants and needs. Being outdoors is one of the ways that you can relax and remember who you really are.

How this color benefits you:
Your personal color gives you the strength to move through the complexities of life. Wearing, meditating on, or surrounding yourself with Green-Blue Slate reminds you to take care of yourself as you interact with others.

Compatible birthdays:
May 30 • August 6 • November 19

Green-Blue Slate = PANTONE 17-5117

BLUE HEAVEN

MUSICAL
PROMOTER
SEXY

If you were born on this day:
You are sexy and congenial, and people are drawn to you. You have a natural zest for life, and the room is livelier when you are in it. You have many creative talents that you can channel into music, business, or theater. Try not to let the sensual side of life pull you too far off your purpose. Your desire for expansion and expression needs to be channeled and supported, so that you do not lose your sense of balance.

How this color benefits you:
Wearing, meditating on, or surrounding yourself with Blue Heaven reminds you to live life fully without losing your way back home.

Compatible birthdays:
January 28 • June 18 • October 17

Blue Heaven = PANTONE 17-4023

DECEMBER 15

ENGLISH MANOR

REFLECTIVE
IMAGINATIVE
INNOVATIVE

If you were born on this day:
You have an unusual and often profound take on life. It is your ability to see and hear things differently that sets you apart from others. You can excel in the arts, where your creativity and personal perceptions can lead others into a unique way of experiencing the world. You often succeed in music and philosophy.

How this color benefits you:
Your personal color reminds you to share your thoughts and perceptions with others. Wearing, meditating on, or surrounding yourself with English Manor helps you to maintain your integrity and individuality.

Compatible birthdays:
March 30 • July 19 • July 22

English Manor = PANTONE 17-3920

PURPLE SAGE

PERCEPTIVE
DEEP
STRONG

If you were born on this day:
You have an innate desire to learn and understand things. You are partner-oriented, and it is likely that you will feel best when you are connected closely to another person. It is important for you to know the reason behind things. Your mind is deep and penetrating, and you are not satisfied with superficial answers or people.

How this color benefits you:
Your personal color helps calm your restlessness. Wearing, meditating on, or surrounding yourself with Purple Sage supports your quest for truth and reminds you to have trust in relation to love and commitment.

Compatible birthdays:
January 28 • August 26 • September 12

Purple Sage = PANTONE 18-3712

DECEMBER 18

BLUE SAPPHIRE

ADVENTUROUS
APPEALING
CREATIVE

If you were born on this day:
You can do just about anything you put your mind to. Your ability to laugh and keep your sense of humor is one of the reasons people love to be around you. You have an ability to see things that others often can't see. It is this ability that makes you unique but can also make you feel a bit out of step with the rest of society.

How this color benefits you:
Wearing, meditating on, or surrounding yourself with Blue Sapphire encourages you to be true to yourself without feeling separate and alone.

Compatible birthdays:
March 10 • June 6 • August 10

Blue Sapphire = PANTONE 18-4231

LAGOON

REGAL
EXPRESSIVE
DETERMINED

If you were born on this day:
You are capable of achieving many of your aspirations through pure determination and will. Some of this strength comes from the challenges you may have faced while growing up. Once you make up your mind to do something, you have the necessary stamina to accomplish your aims. You may end up being in the public eye.

How this color benefits you:
Your personal color reminds you to infuse your life with optimism and enthusiasm. Wearing, meditating on, or surrounding yourself with Lagoon helps you live life in a balanced and wondrous way.

Compatible birthdays:
March 12 • April 9 • May 17

Lagoon = PANTONE 16-5418

PARISIAN BLUE

SENSITIVE
STRONG
SPIRITUAL

If you were born on this day:
You have great hunches and are a kind and loving person. You are far stronger than most people know. Loving and fair, you were born with a giving nature. Resist the urge to doubt yourself when you interact with people who are stingier and more fearful than you are. Move around their energy as you would an iceberg in the sea.

How this color benefits you:
Wearing, meditating on, or surrounding yourself with Parisian Blue reminds you of your destination and your true nature. It is remembering these two things that will enable you to find your way into the heart of happiness.

Compatible birthdays:
January 29 • May 11 • July 31

Parisian Blue = PANTONE 18-4036

CARIBBEAN SEA

PLAYFUL
SMART
ROMANTIC

If you were born on this day:
Your hearty personality is an inspiration to others. You are warm and loving, and everyone seems to want a piece of you. Taking time for yourself is imperative to your well-being and will help you guard against being taken for granted or being pushed and pulled in too many directions. There is far more to you than meets the eye, and there may be times when you feel that few people know the real you.

How this color benefits you:
Wearing, meditating on, or surrounding yourself with Caribbean Sea helps you release negative emotions so that you can feel continually replenished and refreshed.

Compatible birthdays:
April 1 • July 15 • August 30

Caribbean Sea = PANTONE 18-4525

EVERGREEN

SOLID
CREATOR
CONTEMPLATIVE

If you were born on this day:
You have an uncanny ability to build
and persevere once you decide
where you are going and what you
want in life. You need to cultivate
security and material success.
Manifesting your ideas is an important part of your evolution. Trust
and patience will be two of your
strongest allies.

How this color benefits you:
Your personal color reminds you
that being in nature is vital to your
well-being. Wearing, meditating on,
or surrounding yourself with
Evergreen helps you align with
healthy energy and prosperity.

Compatible birthdays:
January 29 • February 10 •
August 3

Evergreen = PANTONE 19-5420

ASPEN GREEN

VISIONARY
POWERFUL
MYSTERIOUS

If you were born on this day:
You have an enterprising spirit and can capitalize on your talents. Although you can be friendly and good-natured, much of your personality and feelings remain hidden from the outside world. Money and power often come easily to you as you focus and make your mark in the world. It is important for you to feel that you are doing something meaningful and that you are connected to something bigger than yourself.

How this color benefits you:
Wearing, meditating on, or surrounding yourself with Aspen Green helps you stay linked to friends and family as you share your gifts with the world at large.

Compatible birthdays:
April 28 • May 17 • July 17

Aspen Green = PANTONE 17-0215

GREEN SPRUCE

EMOTIONAL
PROPHETIC
MYSTICAL

If you were born on this day:
You are sensual and alluring, and people are drawn to you. You need creative outlets to express yourself so that life doesn't become too dramatic. There are times when you may have to face a lot of responsibilities. Some of these can be overwhelming if you do not have a secure foundation and a strong spiritual connection.

How this color benefits you:
Your personal color helps you stay encouraged and optimistic. Wearing, meditating on, or surrounding yourself with Green Spruce reminds you to share your talents so that you feel useful and productive.

Compatible birthdays:
January 23 • February 28 • November 15

Green Spruce = PANTONE 16-5820

HUNTER GREEN

DETERMINED
UNUSUAL
GOAL-ORIENTED

If you were born on this day:
You were born with a nice mix of intuition and practicality. It is important for you to feel financially secure and grounded. No amount of wealth, status, or achievement will be enough if you have not culti-vated the spiritual side of your nature. Stability, home, and love are all very important to you. You are loyal, dependable, and giving, once you have accepted a person into your intimate circle.

How this color benefits you:
Your personal color reminds you to stay connected to the spiritual side of life. Wearing, meditating on, or surrounding yourself with Hunter Green helps calm any financial or mundane worries you may feel.

Compatible birthdays:
March 24 • May 29 • October 10

Hunter Green = PANTONE 19-5511

DECEMBER 25

LARKSPUR

COMPLEX
COURAGEOUS
RESTLESS

If you were born on this day:
It is best for you to be in a position of authority. It is not a great idea for you to follow someone else's rules. Courageous and complex, you are not always easily understood. You want to know what makes things tick. You are concerned about the core of a situation, not the appearance of things. Part of your challenge is to learn how to work with a partner. Receptivity and diplomacy are needed in your exchanges with others.

How this color benefits you:
Wearing, meditating on, or surrounding yourself with the color Larkspur helps you combine your depth with subtlety and grace.

Compatible birthdays:
February 10 • March 20 • July 12

Larkspur = PANTONE 17-4421

TURKISH TILE

PROTECTIVE
IDEALISTIC
EXPRESSIVE

DECEMBER 27

If you were born on this day:
Your mind is sharp and discriminating.
Although you are capable of making
good judgments, there are times
when you are idealistic about relationships. Be sure to connect
with people who love and support
you. You have a unique way of
expressing yourself, and people find
you interesting and distinctive. You
have a dry sense of humor that
shows off your quick intellect and
perception.

How this color benefits you:
Wearing, meditating on, or
surrounding yourself with Turkish
Tile helps you stay lighthearted and
inspired while reminding you to
believe in yourself and others.

Compatible birthdays:
March 28 • August 12 •
November 19

Turkish Tile = PANTONE 18-4432

VIRIDIAN GREEN

QUICK
SOPHISTICATED
CAPABLE

If you were born on this day:
Born to lead and inspire, you do well at the head of the class. You are charismatic and self-assured and can move through different parts of society with ease and confidence. Most people born on this day are hardworking and driven. Try not to let your confidence and sense of purpose lead you to doing everything yourself. Security and a sense of belonging are important to your well-being.

How this color benefits you:
Your personal color helps you stay flexible and open to the unexpected. Wearing, meditating on, or surrounding yourself with Viridian Green helps you guard against being stubborn or emotionally unavailable.

Compatible birthdays:
April 13 • July 19 • October 1

Viridian Green = PANTONE 17-5126

PURPLE HAZE

TALENTED
VERSATILE
SPIRITUAL

If you were born on this day:
Talented and versatile, you are a great entertainer. Your natural spunk makes you a favorite at any social function. Although you can appear outgoing, you are also very sensitive, and have a need to retreat and re-energize. The challenge of having two very different qualities can at times feel overwhelming. The desire to be alone, coupled with the need for a mate, is another challenge you sometimes face.

How this color benefits you:
Your personal color helps you step forward with confidence. Wearing, meditating on, or surrounding yourself with Purple Haze allows you to join with another person without the fear of losing your individuality.

Compatible birthdays:
February 29 • August 5 • November 15

Purple Haze = PANTONE 18-3718

SUNBURN

ARTIST
COMMUNICATOR
STORYTELLER

If you were born on this day:
Your ability to make people stand up and take notice is one of your many gifts. You are able to convey ideas and opinions to the masses. Communicating life's truths is one of your many pleasures. You are unique and colorful, and people don't often forget you once they have met you. Your verbal agility is quite rare.

How this color benefits you:
Wearing, meditating on, or surrounding yourself with Sunburn helps you channel the creative and sensitive side of your personality in a healthy and balanced manner.

Compatible birthdays:
February 15 • June 29 • September 3

Sunburn = PANTONE 16-1429

BRITTANY BLUE

POWERFUL
CHARISMATIC
REGAL

DECEMBER 31

If you were born on this day:
Your talent and power are quite exceptional but is not always easy to handle. A strong base is needed to support your energy and drive. Discipline, intention, and love must be present to achieve your goals with a feeling of peace and accomplishment.

How this color benefits you:
Your personal color resonates with gratitude and humility. Wearing, meditating on, or surrounding yourself with Brittany Blue helps dissolve the lines of separation and loneliness that people sometimes feel. It reminds you to appreciate your gifts and helps you feel connected to the world.

Compatible birthdays:
April 18 • June 19 • July 31

Brittany Blue = PANTONE 18-5610

PERSONAL COLOR SWATCHES

Use the following perforated color swatches to take your
personal daily and monthly colors with you all the time—
when traveling, shopping, or just out and about.

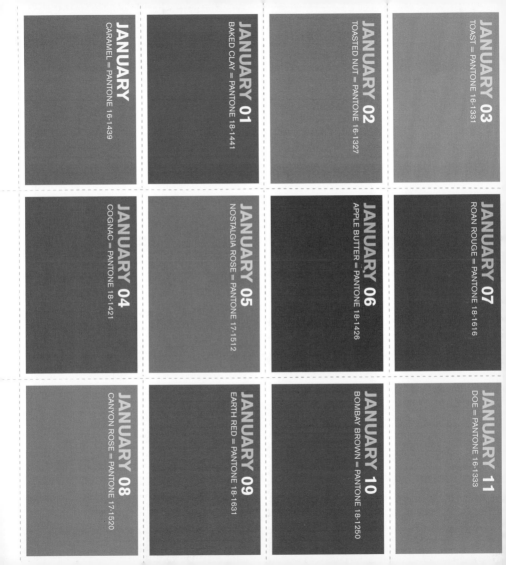

JANUARY
CARAMEL = PANTONE 16-1439

JANUARY 01
BAKED CLAY = PANTONE 18-1441

JANUARY 02
TOASTED NUT = PANTONE 16-1327

JANUARY 03
TOAST = PANTONE 16-1331

JANUARY 04
COGNAC = PANTONE 18-1421

JANUARY 05
NOSTALGIA ROSE = PANTONE 17-1512

JANUARY 06
APPLE BUTTER = PANTONE 18-1426

JANUARY 07
ROAN ROUGE = PANTONE 18-1616

JANUARY 08
CANYON ROSE = PANTONE 17-1520

JANUARY 09
EARTH RED = PANTONE 18-1631

JANUARY 10
BOMBAY BROWN = PANTONE 18-1250

JANUARY 11
DOE = PANTONE 16-1333

JANUARY 12
GINGER BREAD = PANTONE 18-1244

JANUARY 13
FIR = PANTONE 18-5621

JANUARY 14
ARCTIC = PANTONE 17-4911

JANUARY 15
CEDAR WOOD = PANTONE 17-1525

JANUARY 16
BURLWOOD = PANTONE 17-1516

JANUARY 17
TANDORI SPICE = PANTONE 18-1444

JANUARY 18
DECO ROSE = PANTONE 17-1614

JANUARY 19
LION = PANTONE 17-1330

JANUARY 20
LIGHT MAHOGANY = PANTONE 18-1436

JANUARY 21
ZEPHYR = PANTONE 15-1906

JANUARY 22
BLUE SURF = PANTONE 16-5106

JANUARY 23
PURPLE IMPRESSION = PANTONE 17-3919

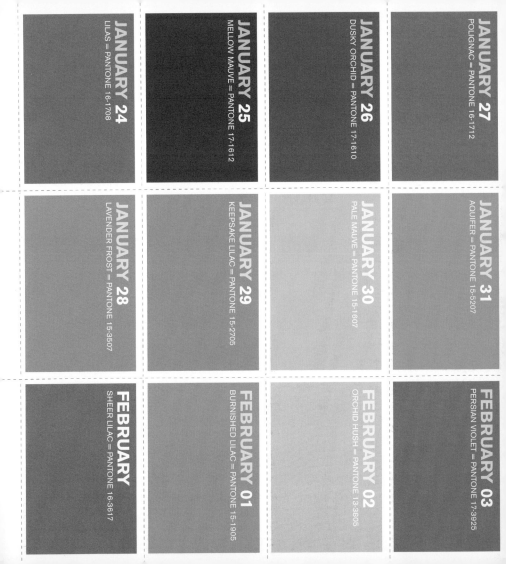

JANUARY 24
LILAS = PANTONE 16-1708

JANUARY 25
MELLOW MAUVE = PANTONE 17-1612

JANUARY 26
DUSKY ORCHID = PANTONE 17-1610

JANUARY 27
POLIGNAC = PANTONE 16-1712

JANUARY 28
LAVENDER FROST = PANTONE 15-3507

JANUARY 29
KEEPSAKE LILAC = PANTONE 15-2705

JANUARY 30
PALE MAUVE = PANTONE 15-1607

JANUARY 31
AQUIFER = PANTONE 15-5207

FEBRUARY
SHEER LILAC = PANTONE 16-3617

FEBRUARY 01
BURNISHED LILAC = PANTONE 15-1905

FEBRUARY 02
ORCHID HUSH = PANTONE 13-3805

FEBRUARY 03
PERSIAN VIOLET = PANTONE 17-3925

FEBRUARY 04
CELADON GREEN = PANTONE 14-0114

FEBRUARY 05
LAVENDER LUSTRE = PANTONE 16-3920

FEBRUARY 06
VIOLET = PANTONE 16-3320

FEBRUARY 07
PAISLEY PURPLE = PANTONE 17-3730

FEBRUARY 08
CROCUS = PANTONE 16-3115

FEBRUARY 09
MAUVE SHADOWS = PANTONE 16-3205

FEBRUARY 10
PEACH = PANTONE 14-1227

FEBRUARY 11
VIOLET TULIP = PANTONE 16-3823

FEBRUARY 12
WISTERIA = PANTONE 16-3810

FEBRUARY 13
LAUREL GREEN = PANTONE 15-6313

FEBRUARY 14
VISTA BLUE = PANTONE 15-3930

FEBRUARY 15
LUPINE = PANTONE 16-3521

FEBRUARY 16
LAVENDULA = PANTONE 15-3620

FEBRUARY 17
DUSTY LAVENDER = PANTONE 17-3313

FEBRUARY 18
ORCHID HAZE = PANTONE 16-2107

FEBRUARY 19
BLUSH = PANTONE 15-1614

FEBRUARY 20
LAVENDER AURA = PANTONE 16-3911

FEBRUARY 21
LAVENDER MIST = PANTONE 16-3307

FEBRUARY 22
CAMEO GREEN = PANTONE 14-6312

FEBRUARY 23
FOREVER BLUE = PANTONE 16-4019

FEBRUARY 24
PINK NECTAR = PANTONE 14-2305

FEBRUARY 25
SWEET LAVENDER = PANTONE 16-3931

FEBRUARY 26
CHALK VIOLET = PANTONE 17-3615

FEBRUARY 27
VIOLET QUARTZ = PANTONE 18-1720

FEBRUARY 28
ORCHID MIST = PANTONE 17-3612

FEBRUARY 29
ASHLEY BLUE = PANTONE 16-4013

MARCH
FAIR AQUA = PANTONE 12-5409

MARCH 01
PISTACHIO GREEN = PANTONE 13-0221

MARCH 02
BAY = PANTONE 12-5507

MARCH 03
ROSE TAN = PANTONE 16-1511

MARCH 04
RESEDA = PANTONE 15-6414

MARCH 05
BLUE LIGHT = PANTONE 13-4909

MARCH 06
PASTEL LAVENDER = PANTONE 14-3209

MARCH 07
DAWN PINK = PANTONE 15-2205

MARCH 08
MAUVE MIST = PANTONE 15-3207

MARCH 09
MELLOW ROSE = PANTONE 15-1515

MARCH 10
MELLOW GREEN = PANTONE 12-0426

MARCH 11
WINTER SKY = PANTONE 14-4307

MARCH 12
ALMOST APRICOT = PANTONE 15-1319

MARCH 13
PASTEL GREEN = PANTONE 13-0116

MARCH 14
MISTY LILAC = PANTONE 15-3807

MARCH 15
CASHMERE BLUE = PANTONE 14-4115

MARCH 16
THISTLE = PANTONE 14-3907

MARCH 17
VIOLET TULLE = PANTONE 16-3416

MARCH 18
MUTED CLAY = PANTONE 16-1330

MARCH 19
ARCADIAN GREEN = PANTONE 14-0123

MARCH 20
DUSTY JADE GREEN = PANTONE 15-5711

MARCH 21
BASIL = PANTONE 16-6216

MARCH 22
PURPLE ASH = PANTONE 17-3810

MARCH 23
STORM BLUE = PANTONE 17-4716

MARCH 24
MAUVEWOOD = PANTONE 17-1522

MARCH 25
BERRY CONSERVE = PANTONE 18-3013

MARCH 26
WISTFUL MAUVE = PANTONE 17-1511

MARCH 27
BRUSCHETTA = PANTONE 18-1346

MARCH 28
SIERRA = PANTONE 18-1239

MARCH 29
OIL BLUE = PANTONE 17-5111

MARCH 30
FADED ROSE = PANTONE 18-1629

MARCH 31
JACARANDA = PANTONE 17-3930

APRIL
CAYENNE = PANTONE 18-1651

APRIL 01
FIERY RED = PANTONE 18-1664

APRIL 05
ORANGE.COM = PANTONE 18-1561

APRIL 04
TRUE RED = PANTONE 19-1664

APRIL 03
CHERRY TOMATO = PANTONE 17-1563

APRIL 02
RAPTURE ROSE = PANTONE 17-1929

APRIL 09
POPPY RED = PANTONE 17-1664

APRIL 08
SKI PATROL = PANTONE 18-1761

APRIL 07
SKYWAY = PANTONE 14-4112

APRIL 06
BEETROOT PURPLE = PANTONE 18-2143

APRIL 13
ROCOCCO RED = PANTONE 18-1652

APRIL 12
GERANIUM = PANTONE 17-1753

APRIL 11
SANGRIA = PANTONE 19-2047

APRIL 10
VERMILLION ORANGE = PANTONE 16-1362

APRIL 14
HIBISCUS = PANTONE 18-1762

APRIL 15
CERISE = PANTONE 19-1955

APRIL 16
VIRTUAL PINK = PANTONE 18-1856

APRIL 17
RIBBON RED = PANTONE 19-1663

APRIL 18
CRIMSON = PANTONE 19-1762

APRIL 19
HIGH RISK RED = PANTONE 18-1763

APRIL 20
AFRICAN VIOLET = PANTONE 16-3520

APRIL 21
OPERA MAUVE = PANTONE 16-3116

APRIL 22
DARK PURPLE = PANTONE 19-2524

APRIL 23
LAVENDER HERB = PANTONE 16-3310

APRIL 24
ULTRAMARINE = PANTONE 17-4037

APRIL 25
AZURE BLUE = PANTONE 17-4139

APRIL 26
IBIS ROSE = PANTONE 17-2520

APRIL 27
EASTER EGG = PANTONE 16-3925

APRIL 28
NORTH SEA = PANTONE 18-5115

APRIL 29
DEEP PERIWINKLE = PANTONE 17-3932

APRIL 30
ASTER PURPLE = PANTONE 17-3826

MAY
BUD GREEN = PANTONE 15-6442

MAY 01
SHAMROCK = PANTONE 15-6432

MAY 02
SHALE GREEN = PANTONE 16-6116

MAY 03
JUNIPER = PANTONE 18-6330

MAY 04
VINEYARD GREEN = PANTONE 18-0117

MAY 05
KELLY GREEN = PANTONE 16-6138

MAY 06
GREEN EYES = PANTONE 16-0224

MAY 07
CRÈME DE MENTHE = PANTONE 16-5919

MAY 08
GARDEN GREEN = PANTONE 19-0230

MAY 09
WINTER GREEN = PANTONE 16-5924

MAY 10
KIWI = PANTONE 16-0235

MAY 11
GREEN TEA = PANTONE 15-6428

MAY 12
CALLA GREEN = PANTONE 18-0435

MAY 13
PIQUANT GREEN = PANTONE 17-0235

MAY 14
DEEP MINT = PANTONE 17-5937

MAY 15
LAVENDER GRAY = PANTONE 17-3910

MAY 16
WOODROSE = PANTONE 16-1806

MAY 17
HENNA = PANTONE 19-1334

MAY 18
WITHERED ROSE = PANTONE 18-1435

MAY 19
APRICOT TAN = PANTONE 15-1237

MAY 20
SMOKE GREEN = PANTONE 15-6315

MAY 21
MANDARIN ORANGE = PANTONE 16-1459

MAY 22
PERIDOT = PANTONE 17-0336

MAY 23
HOLLY GREEN = PANTONE 16-5932

MAY 24
SEEDLING = PANTONE 14-0217

MAY 25
NILE GREEN = PANTONE 14-0121

MAY 26
PEACH BEIGE = PANTONE 15-1516

MAY 27
DILL = PANTONE 18-0108

MAY 28
BUTTERSCOTCH = PANTONE 15-1147

MAY 29
PASTEL LILAC = PANTONE 14-3812

MAY 30
BURNT ORANGE = PANTONE 16-1448

MAY 31
GRASSHOPPER = PANTONE 18-0332

JUNE
ASPEN GOLD = PANTONE 13-0850

JUNE 01
DAFFODIL = PANTONE 14-0850

JUNE 02
NILE = PANTONE 14-0223

JUNE 03
PUMPKIN = PANTONE 14-1139

JUNE 04
GREEN GLOW = PANTONE 13-0442

JUNE 05
MING = PANTONE 15-6120

JUNE 06
CORAL REEF = PANTONE 15-1331

JUNE 07
VIOLET ICE = PANTONE 15-2706

JUNE 08
GOLDEN APRICOT = PANTONE 14-1041

JUNE 09
AMBERLIGHT = PANTONE 14-1217

JUNE 10
GOLDEN NUGGET = PANTONE 16-1142

JUNE 11
SUNSET GOLD = PANTONE 13-0940

JUNE 12
BIRD OF PARADISE = PANTONE 16-1357

JUNE 13
BRIGHT CHARTREUSE = PANTONE 14-0445

JUNE 14
SPRING BOUQUET = PANTONE 14-6340

JUNE 15
APRICOT NECTAR = PANTONE 14-1133

JUNE 16
RAFFIA = PANTONE 13-0725

JUNE 17
CANYON SUNSET = PANTONE 15-1333

JUNE 18
BRANDIED MELON = PANTONE 16-1340

JUNE 19
GOLDEN OCHRE = PANTONE 16-1346

JUNE 20
LETTUCE GREEN = PANTONE 13-0324

JUNE 21
CHAMOIS = PANTONE 15-1145

JUNE 22
BRIGHT LIME GREEN = PANTONE 14-0244

JUNE 23
BRIGHT AQUA = PANTONE 16-5422

JUNE 24
TIGERLILY = PANTONE 17-1456

JUNE 25
GULL GRAY = PANTONE 16-3803

JUNE 26
RAW SIENNA = PANTONE 17-1436

JUNE 27
CRABAPPLE = PANTONE 16-1532

JUNE 28
ORANGE OCHRE = PANTONE 16-1253

JUNE 29
FOREST SHADE = PANTONE 15-6423

JUNE 30
CADMIUM ORANGE = PANTONE 15-1340

JULY
CORAL BLUSH = PANTONE 14-1909

JULY 01
PALE BLUSH = PANTONE 14-1312

JULY 02
FRAGRANT LILAC = PANTONE 14-3204

JULY 03
SHELL CORAL = PANTONE 15-1334

JULY 04
LILY GREEN = PANTONE 13-0317

JULY 05
AQUATIC = PANTONE 14-4510

JULY 06
FAIR ORCHID = PANTONE 15-3508

JULY 07
PERSIAN JEWEL = PANTONE 17-3934

JULY 08
LILAC MARBLE = PANTONE 14-3903

JULY 09
SILVER PINK = PANTONE 14-1508

JULY 10
APRICOT ICE = PANTONE 13-1020

JULY 11
POTPOURRI = PANTONE 13-2004

JULY 12
PEACH PINK = PANTONE 15-1530

JULY 13
SEAFOAM GREEN = PANTONE 12-0313

JULY 14
DELPHINIUM BLUE = PANTONE 16-4519

JULY 15
MOONLITE MAUVE = PANTONE 16-2614

JULY 16
BRANDIED APRICOT = PANTONE 16-1610

JULY 17
IRIS = PANTONE 14-3805

JULY 18
TERRA COTTA = PANTONE 16-1526

JULY 19
TANGERINE = PANTONE 15-1247

JULY 20
BUTTERFLY = PANTONE 12-0322

JULY 21
AMBERGLOW = PANTONE 16-1350

JULY 22
OPALINE GREEN = PANTONE 14-0226

JULY 23
NILE BLUE = PANTONE 15-5210

JULY 24
MELON = PANTONE 16-1442

JULY 25
WEDGEWOOD = PANTONE 18-3935

JULY 26
SPICED CORAL = PANTONE 17-1644

JULY 27
FIESTA = PANTONE 17-1564

JULY 28
CORAL ROSE = PANTONE 16-1349

JULY 29
LITTLE BOY BLUE = PANTONE 16-4132

JULY 30
NECTARINE = PANTONE 16-1360

JULY 31
BEECHNUT = PANTONE 14-0425

AUGUST
SUN ORANGE = PANTONE 16-1257

AUGUST 01
AUTUMN SUNSET = PANTONE 16-1343

AUGUST 02
CADMIUM YELLOW = PANTONE 15-1054

AUGUST 03
FIRECRACKER = PANTONE 16-1452

AUGUST 04
SUNFLOWER = PANTONE 16-1054

AUGUST 05
FELDSPAR = PANTONE 16-5815

AUGUST 06
CAMELLIA = PANTONE 16-1541

AUGUST 07
ASH ROSE = PANTONE 17-1514

AUGUST 08
AZALEA = PANTONE 17-1842

AUGUST 09
GOLDEN POPPY = PANTONE 16-1462

AUGUST 10
ARTISAN'S GOLD = PANTONE 15-1049

AUGUST 11
GOLD EARTH = PANTONE 15-1234

AUGUST 12
FLAMINGO = PANTONE 16-1450

AUGUST 13
APRICOT ORANGE = PANTONE 17-1353

AUGUST 14
TEAL BLUE = PANTONE 17-5024

AUGUST 15
STONEWASH = PANTONE 17-3917

AUGUST 16
WILD ROSE = PANTONE 16-1715

AUGUST 17
MECCA ORANGE = PANTONE 18-1450

AUGUST 18
RUST = PANTONE 18-1248

AUGUST 19
VIBRANT ORANGE = PANTONE 16-1364

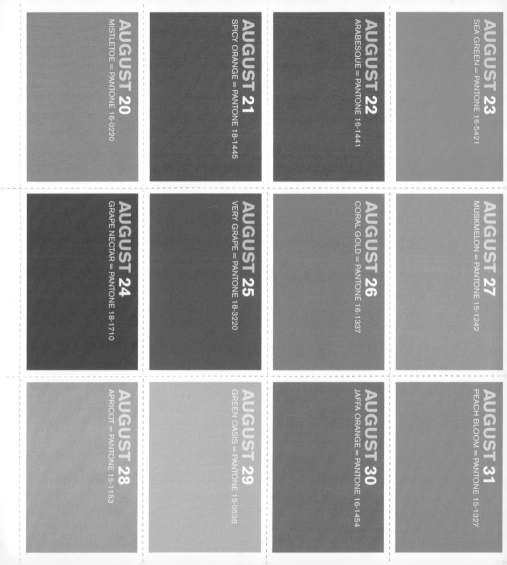

AUGUST 20
MISTLETOE = PANTONE 16-0220

AUGUST 21
SPICY ORANGE = PANTONE 18-1445

AUGUST 22
ARABESQUE = PANTONE 16-1441

AUGUST 23
SEA GREEN = PANTONE 16-5421

AUGUST 24
GRAPE NECTAR = PANTONE 18-1710

AUGUST 25
VERY GRAPE = PANTONE 18-3220

AUGUST 26
CORAL GOLD = PANTONE 16-1337

AUGUST 27
MUSKMELON = PANTONE 15-1242

AUGUST 28
APRICOT = PANTONE 15-1153

AUGUST 29
GREEN OASIS = PANTONE 15-0538

AUGUST 30
JAFFA ORANGE = PANTONE 16-1454

AUGUST 31
PEACH BLOOM = PANTONE 15-1327

SEPTEMBER
BAJA BLUE = PANTONE 18-3946

SEPTEMBER 01
SMOKE BLUE = PANTONE 17-4412

SEPTEMBER 02
DAYBREAK = PANTONE 17-3817

SEPTEMBER 03
GRAPEADE = PANTONE 18-3211

SEPTEMBER 04
AQUA = PANTONE 15-4717

SEPTEMBER 05
NEPTUNE GREEN = PANTONE 14-6017

SEPTEMBER 06
VERONICA = PANTONE 18-3834

SEPTEMBER 07
DAHLIA PURPLE = PANTONE 17-3834

SEPTEMBER 08
ETRUSCAN RED = PANTONE 18-1434

SEPTEMBER 09
GRAPE ROYALE = PANTONE 19-3518

SEPTEMBER 10
JADESHEEN = PANTONE 16-6324

SEPTEMBER 11
INFINITY = PANTONE 17-4015

SEPTEMBER 12
MEADOW = PANTONE 14-6319

SEPTEMBER 13
BERYL GREEN = PANTONE 16-5515

SEPTEMBER 14
HORIZON BLUE = PANTONE 16-4427

SEPTEMBER 15
TULIPWOOD = PANTONE 18-1709

SEPTEMBER 16
ELDERBERRY = PANTONE 17-1605

SEPTEMBER 17
TABASCO = PANTONE 18-1536

SEPTEMBER 18
AUTUMN LEAF = PANTONE 17-1347

SEPTEMBER 19
CACTUS = PANTONE 18-0130

SEPTEMBER 20
SILT GREEN = PANTONE 14-5706

SEPTEMBER 21
GRAPE SHAKE = PANTONE 18-2109

SEPTEMBER 22
MISTY ROSE = PANTONE 15-1512

SEPTEMBER 23
SKY BLUE = PANTONE 14-4318

SEPTEMBER 24
CORNFLOWER BLUE = PANTONE 16-4031

SEPTEMBER 25
SEA FOG = PANTONE 16-3304

SEPTEMBER 26
PLUM WINE = PANTONE 18-1411

SEPTEMBER 27
RENAISSANCE ROSE = PANTONE 18-1613

SEPTEMBER 28
BOK CHOY = PANTONE 13-6208

SEPTEMBER 29
DREAM BLUE = PANTONE 15-4005

SEPTEMBER 30
DUSK = PANTONE 17-3812

OCTOBER
CERULEAN = PANTONE 15-4020

OCTOBER 01
PURPLE HEATHER = PANTONE 14-3911

OCTOBER 02
KENTUCKY BLUE = PANTONE 15-3915

OCTOBER 03
ORCHID BOUQUET = PANTONE 15-3412

OCTOBER 04
HEATHER = PANTONE 14-4110

OCTOBER 05
WINSOME ORCHID = PANTONE 14-3206

OCTOBER 06
GRAPEMIST = PANTONE 16-3929

OCTOBER 07
LANGUID LAVENDER = PANTONE 15-3910

OCTOBER 08
MULBERRY = PANTONE 17-3014

OCTOBER 09
SMOKY GRAPE = PANTONE 16-3110

OCTOBER 10
DUSTY PINK = PANTONE 14-1316

OCTOBER 11
VIOLA = PANTONE 16-3815

OCTOBER 12
EGGSHELL BLUE = PANTONE 14-4809

OCTOBER 13
OPAL BLUE = PANTONE 12-5406

OCTOBER 14
STARLIGHT BLUE = PANTONE 12-4609

OCTOBER 15
LILAC SNOW = PANTONE 13-3405

OCTOBER 16
LAVENDER = PANTONE 15-3817

OCTOBER 17
ORCHID SMOKE = PANTONE 15-2210

OCTOBER 18
LIGHT LILAC = PANTONE 12-2903

OCTOBER 19
BURNT CORAL = PANTONE 16-1529

OCTOBER 20
COSMIC SKY = PANTONE 15-3909

OCTOBER 21
CHINTZ ROSE = PANTONE 13-1408

OCTOBER 22
DUSTY AQUA = PANTONE 12-5506

OCTOBER 23
HEIRLOOM LILAC = PANTONE 16-3812

OCTOBER 24
REGAL ORCHID = PANTONE 16-3525

OCTOBER 25
RED VIOLET = PANTONE 17-1818

OCTOBER 26
BARBERRY = PANTONE 18-1760

OCTOBER 27
MOLTEN LAVA = PANTONE 18-1555

OCTOBER 28
BAROQUE ROSE = PANTONE 18-1634

OCTOBER 29
BEAUJOLAIS = PANTONE 18-2027

OCTOBER 30
CARDINAL = PANTONE 18-1643

OCTOBER 31
TIBETAN RED = PANTONE 19-1934

NOVEMBER
CLARET RED = PANTONE 17-1740

NOVEMBER 01
MARS RED = PANTONE 18-1655

NOVEMBER 02
RASPBERRY WINE = PANTONE 18-1741

NOVEMBER 03
CHINESE RED = PANTONE 18-1663

NOVEMBER 04
AMERICAN BEAUTY = PANTONE 19-1759

NOVEMBER 05
JESTER RED = PANTONE 19-1862

NOVEMBER 06
DEEP CLARET = PANTONE 19-1840

NOVEMBER 07
CHILI PEPPER = PANTONE 19-1557

NOVEMBER 08
RED BUD = PANTONE 19-1850

NOVEMBER 09
PERSIAN RED = PANTONE 19-1860

NOVEMBER 10
AURORA RED = PANTONE 18-1550

NOVEMBER 11
MALAGA = PANTONE 17-1723

NOVEMBER 12
BAKED APPLE = PANTONE 18-1648

NOVEMBER 13
MAGENTA HAZE = PANTONE 18-2525

NOVEMBER 14
RED CLAY = PANTONE 18-1454

NOVEMBER 15
GARNET ROSE = PANTONE 18-1633

NOVEMBER 16
SLATE ROSE = PANTONE 18-1635

NOVEMBER 17
POMPEIAN RED = PANTONE 18-1658

NOVEMBER 18
AMARANTH = PANTONE 19-2410

NOVEMBER 19
RED OCHRE = PANTONE 18-1442

NOVEMBER 20
ROSE WINE = PANTONE 17-1623

NOVEMBER 21
GARNET = PANTONE 19-1655

NOVEMBER 22
HEATHER ROSE = PANTONE 17-1608

NOVEMBER 23
BORDEAUX = PANTONE 17-1710

NOVEMBER 24
DRY ROSE = PANTONE 18-1725

NOVEMBER 25
MAUVE ORCHID = PANTONE 16-2111

NOVEMBER 26
VALERIAN = PANTONE 17-3410

NOVEMBER 27
THISTLE DOWN = PANTONE 16-3930

NOVEMBER 28
ARAGON = PANTONE 17-1532

NOVEMBER 29
LAVENDER VIOLET = PANTONE 17-3924

NOVEMBER 30
SAXONY BLUE = PANTONE 18-4225

DECEMBER
PAGODA BLUE = PANTONE 17-4724

DECEMBER 01
BAYOU = PANTONE 18-5121

DECEMBER 02
ADRIATIC BLUE = PANTONE 17-4320

DECEMBER 03
CELESTIAL = PANTONE 18-4530

DECEMBER 04
CANTON = PANTONE 16-5112

DECEMBER 05
RIVIERA = PANTONE 17-4027

DECEMBER 06
DUSK BLUE = PANTONE 16-4120

DECEMBER 07
CENDRE BLUE = PANTONE 17-4131

DECEMBER 08
ORIENT BLUE = PANTONE 19-3947

DECEMBER 09
VELVET MORNING = PANTONE 18-3927

DECEMBER 10
PORCELAIN GREEN = PANTONE 17-5421

DECEMBER 11
DELFT = PANTONE 19-4039

DECEMBER 12
LYONS BLUE = PANTONE 19-4340

DECEMBER 13
GALAPAGOS GREEN = PANTONE 18-5725

DECEMBER 14
GREEN-BLUE SLATE = PANTONE 17-5117

DECEMBER 15
BLUE HEAVEN = PANTONE 17-4023

DECEMBER 16
ENGLISH MANOR = PANTONE 17-3920

DECEMBER 17
PURPLE SAGE = PANTONE 18-3712

DECEMBER 18
BLUE SAPPHIRE = PANTONE 18-4231

DECEMBER 19
LAGOON = PANTONE 16-5418

DECEMBER 20
PARISIAN BLUE = PANTONE 18-4036

DECEMBER 21
CARIBBEAN SEA = PANTONE 18-4525

DECEMBER 22
EVERGREEN = PANTONE 19-5420

DECEMBER 23
ASPEN GREEN = PANTONE 17-0215

DECEMBER 24
GREEN SPRUCE = PANTONE 16-5820

DECEMBER 25
HUNTER GREEN = PANTONE 19-5511

DECEMBER 26
LARKSPUR = PANTONE 17-4421

DECEMBER 27
TURKISH TILE = PANTONE 18-4432

DECEMBER 28
VIRIDIAN GREEN = PANTONE 17-5126

DECEMBER 29
PURPLE HAZE = PANTONE 18-3718

DECEMBER 30
SUNBURN = PANTONE 16-1429

DECEMBER 31
BRITTANY BLUE = PANTONE 18-5610